WORDS IN SEASON

WORDS IN SEASON

ON SHARING THE HOPE THAT IS WITHIN US

LEON BROWN

Gospel Rich Books
Spotsylvania, Virginia

ISBN 978-0615904726
ISBN 0615904726

www.gospelrichbooks.com

Cover design by David Araujo.
D. Araujo: dnadavid77@gmail.com

First printing 2013.

Printed in the United States of America.

To all my brothers and sisters who desire to make Jesus Christ known

What People Are Saying About

Words in Season

Leon Brown has written one of the most practical applications of how to winsomely share the Good News of the Gospel of our Lord Jesus Christ in a post-modern context. His balance of the theological and a step-by-step approach to the work of the evangelist in the context of the Church is well balanced, saturated with examples, and highly motivational. *Words in Season* is a welcomed addition to my practical theology library.

Jim Bland, Mission to North America Coordinator

Most people I know who struggle in sharing their faith usually ask for three things: prayer, encouragement, and example. With pastoral encouragement and practical example, Leon Brown has given a gem of a little book on evangelism to the church. All of us who find ourselves praying for encouragement to share the faith regularly will find it in these pages. Read it and share it!

Anthony Carter, Author of Blood Work: How the Blood of Christ Accomplishes Our Salvation

Moving from theology to a practical hands on aid, Leon Brown combines his passion for Christ's redeeming work and the hard fought lessons he has learned without confusing the two. *Words in Season* is a timely book in the landscape of Reformed writing whose tendency is to be ingrown. I was blessed to read his passion for evangelism on every page.

Elyse Fitzpatrick, *Author of Found in Him: The Joy of the Incarnation and Our Union with Christ*

In this discussion Leon Brown provides relevant doctrinal foundations and easy conversational openers for those who are apprehensive about personal evangelism. A most helpful study about bearing witness to Jesus Christ.

Hywel Jones, *Professor of Practical Theology, Westminster Seminary California*

Leon Brown writes with a compassion and refreshing perspective that will encourage the body of Christ to remember the importance of day to day evangelism. You will be inspired by his stories of friendly approaches that never compromise the message of the gospel.

Peter Jones, *Executive Director of truthXchange*

In *Words in Season* Leon Brown met his goal of equipping "Christians, at a basic level, with some of the ins and outs of personal evangelism" and leaving the reader encouraged. The book makes personal evangelism feel accessible. It reminds you of biblical truths you already know and which are reinforced regularly at church. Perhaps most importantly, *Words in Season* helps you see that a conversation about church and the gospel can be started naturally and simply. It gives you hope that you are "only one small step from entering into a conversation about spiritual matters."

Richard R. Gerber, *Associate General Secretary of the Committee on Home Missions and Church Extension of the Orthodox Presbyterian Church*

Leon Brown is passionate about Christ and his Church. *Words in Season: On Sharing the Hope that is Within Us* is written with pastoral warmth. Pastor Brown understands the various struggles that are involved when sharing one's faith. *Words in Season* is theologically rich, accessible and a helpful treatment on personal evangelism.

Ronald Johnson, *Christian Hip-Hop Recording Artist, Through Hymn*

Evangelism without the Evangel? Christianity without the Church? All too often oxymorons like this define biblical faith in the 21st century. Leon Brown has written a book that puts the Church and the Gospel at the center of the believer's calling to be witnesses for Christ. He gives comfort and joy to those who worry they lack the gifts or ability to lead the lost to Christ.

Brian Lee, *Pastor of Christ Reformed Church*

Rev. Brown has written an insightful, practical and very much needed book for the church today. Far (and thankfully) from being just another how to book, *Words In Season* speaks to the motivation and blessing of declaring the most important message anyone will ever hear. Among the strengths of *Words In Season* is its accessibility to believers across all maturity levels. Churches would do well to make good use of this as part of their regular discipleship curriculum.

Lance Lewis, *Pastor of Soaring Oaks Presbyterian Church*

Words in Season is a very practical book. I love the examples used by Pastor Brown as any and everybody can utilize his suggestions in witnessing. I highly recommend this book!

Evangel, *Hip-Hop Recording Artist, Christcentric*

Sometimes the Lord brings a small book your way that transforms your life because it was written by someone whose life embodies the subject of the book. Leon Brown starts with God and His church. Then he gently deals with our excuses and fears, and thus practically prepares us to joyfully do the work of personal evangelism. Anyone who knows Leon Brown will know that he oozes with love for the gospel and a desire to get it out to those who need to hear it. So, when he writes about personal evangelism, you had better sit up and listen!

Conrad Mbewe, *Pastor of Kabwata Baptist Church in Lusaka, Zambia*

If you desire to share your faith, but you're struggling with fear, this book is for you. Leon Brown shares his experiences and his wisdom about personal evangelism from a biblical perspective. As you read this book you will be encouraged to share the good news of our Lord Jesus Christ.

William (The Apologist) Mendoza, *Hip-Hop Recording Artist, Christcentric*

Leon Brown provides a brotherly, convicting, yet encouraging word designed to help all believers overcome their fears and become salt and light as bearers of the gospel.

James White, *Director of Alpha & Omega Ministries*

As a busy mom, I appreciate the common sense challenge to look at the opportunities afforded by my daily activities to share the Good News of Christ, whether at the grocery store, library, sports practice or zoo. Pastor Brown has a zeal for equipping believers to care about others enough to share what we know, and it shines through as he breaks down the basics of personal evangelism to make it a less daunting endeavor. I would recommend this book to anyone who wants to interact with people in a deeper way for the glory of God.

Amy Ortiz, *Homeschooling Mother of Five*

As a teenager, I live in a gold mine of opportunity: my own generation! Personal evangelism is not just for adults; it's for everyone since Christ is for everyone. *Words in Season: On Sharing the Hope that is Within Us* moved me toward overcoming the fear of sharing my faith. It also soothed my concern about being rejected on account of my faith by reminding me that I don't have to be a seminary-trained theologian to witness; I don't have to know everything; I don't have to have all the answers—ultimately—because it is *Christ who saves* through the gospel. I'm simply a messenger. *Words in Season* refreshed and invigorated me to get out there and share the message of life to those who need it so badly.

Hannah Proctor, *High School Student*

Leon Brown's *Words in Season* is a timely primer on personal evangelism. Warm, personable, and honest this book presents the biblical case for personal evangelism by rooting it clearly in the broad scope of biblical teaching. Brown's style is winsome yet provocative in that he shares his own pitfalls in sharing the gospel and offers his readers clear encouragements to heed the biblical call to share the gospel openly.

This accessible book is grounded in a robust Reformed theological framework, which may be even oxymoronic as many Evangelicals have caricaturized Reformed Christianity as cold toward evangelism. Not so according to Brown who liberally quotes from Reformed confessions and Reformed theologians. Without explicitly writing so, Brown openly challenges Reformed Christians to ease out of their traditional reluctance to personal evangelism. The book is ideal for adult Sunday School classes, and should, with prayerful attention, ignite personal and corporate evangelistic efforts.

Eric Michael Washington, Assistant Professor of History, Calvin College, Grand Rapids, Michigan.

Words in Season is a *personal* evangelism book that dares to center our evangelistic work around the Divine Drama, address cultural barriers to sharing one's faith, and use both law and Gospel in our presentation methods! This is an outstanding resource for equipping the saints to proclaim Christ naturally, boldly, humbly, accurately, and faithfully.

Eric C. Redmond, *Executive Pastoral Assistant and Bible Professor in Residence, New Canaan Baptist Church*

As I began to read *Words in Season* I was a bit disappointed by its simplicity, but then something began to happen. I found that I was being convicted by the Holy Spirit for my lack of zeal for evangelism. In our post-modern times of process and friendship evangelism, where the emphasis is often more on friendship than evangelism, it is refreshing to read a book by a young post-modern who takes us back to our basic calling to tell people about Jesus.

Wy Plummer, *Pastor and Mission to North America African-American Ministries Coordinator*

CONTENTS

Acknowledgements

I struggled to write this book. I often wondered if I could write something I could stand behind. When I wanted to give up, you encouraged me. Thank you, Rosalinda, for standing beside me in this labor of love. To my former professors, R. Scott Clark and Michael Horton: thank you for helping me more fully understand the importance of the local church. To New City Fellowship (PCA; Fredericksburg, VA), Sterling Presbyterian Church (OPC; Sterling, VA), Christ Presbyterian Church (PCA; Temecula, CA), Grace and Peace Presbyterian Church (OPC; California, MD), Covenant Reformed Presbyterian Church (OPC; Mt. Airy, NC), Redeemer Church (OPC; Santa Maria, CA), and Christ Reformed Church (URC; Washington, D.C.): thank you for allowing me to teach these ideas during the Sunday school hour. To my dear brother and friend, Anthony: thank you for listening to me when these ideas were still fresh in my mind. And to John: though I have never met you, I think highly of you. Among many things, you opened the world of publishing by allowing me to write for the magazine you edit. Then, when I was searching for an editor for this book, you volunteered. Thank you! I hope we meet one day.

Foreword
Michael Horton

The greatest gift that you and I possess in Christ is reconciliation with God. Chosen in Christ from all eternity, we are united by the Spirit through the gospel to Christ through faith, which itself is a gift. From this union we receive "every blessing in heavenly places in Christ" (Ephesians 1:3). We'll never be recipients of a comparable gift.

And the best gift we can give is that same gospel by which others can be reconciled to God: joined to Christ, justified, adopted, sanctified, and finally glorified. We cannot redeem anyone. Nor can we raise those who are spiritually dead to life by our clever techniques, charisma, or persuasion. Nevertheless, we can talk. We can communicate the terms of God's peace treaty on his behalf to actual people who are "strangers and aliens" to the commonwealth of God. We can share the message that finally addresses the origin of that nagging but undefined sense of shame, guilt, and alienation and announces the good news that God justifies the ungodly.

If the Triune God has chosen this means—the communication of his Word—for uniting others like us to the incarnate Son, a gospel that has brought us such rich forgiveness and peace with God, then we cannot fail to raise our hand with the prophet Isaiah and say eagerly, "Here I am, LORD, send me!"

But, alas, we often feel somewhat ambivalent about sharing our faith. It's not that we do not believe it, revel in it, and want others to hear it. Perhaps it is because we are naturally shy, at least when it comes to matters that are likely to be controversial. Maybe we have misconceptions about what personal evangelism is, with visions of standing on street-corners holding "Turn or Burn!" signs. It's easy to say, "I'm really glad that others are doing it—somewhere—and I'll even support them financially." Some people work in sales and others prefer a desk job. It's the division of labor, right?

To be sure, Christ called pastors and teachers to give their lives full-time to studying, proclaiming, and applying God's Word. Yet we would never say that this relieves us of any personal responsibility for reading the Bible and prayer. The same is true of personal evangelism.

Raised in churches where personal evangelism was highly programmed, we can often over-react. Especially in a society that is increasingly hostile to any serious claims when it comes to religion, we hear many people say, "I don't preach the gospel; I live it." The most serious problem with this statement is that it misses the point about what the gospel is in the first place. The gospel is not something that you can live. It's an announcement about what someone else lived, died for, and was raised from the dead to secure. We are called to live in the light of the gospel, in a way that commends the gospel. Yet we are ourselves among the sinners who need to hear that good news that we're called to bring to others. We are always the messengers, not the message.

The gospel is an announcement and announcements need heralds.

Some of us may be burned out on the constant call to be disciple-makers and the expectation to "save souls." That can be a paralyzing fear, keeping the bravest among us from taking on such responsibility. But it is a great relief to learn that we cannot save anyone. We cannot bring a single person to saving faith. This is the gift of God. This frees us up to share the gospel in intentional ways as we go about our normal life.

One of the privileges of teaching in a seminary is that I am able to encounter many young people who are zealous to bring the gospel to believer and unbeliever alike. It is not only an encouragement but a challenge for me to be more intentional about taking advantage of opportunities to plant seeds or to water seeds that someone else has planted. Leon Brown is one of those brothers whose head and heart have found a cordial friendship, one who refuses to choose between knowing Christ and making him known. For Leon, there is no point to getting the gospel *right* in our own minds if we don't get the gospel *out* to those who need it. His own zeal in personal evangelism during his seminary years, and now as a pastor, has been a great example to many, including me.

This book is not another guilt-trip. On the contrary, it opens our horizon to a big God who has a big message that he wants the whole world to hear. Filling our sails with the gospel itself, it leaves us drawing our own conclusion, "Here I am, send me!"

Beyond the motivation, *Words in Season* helps us with the nuts and bolts of evangelistic conversations. Many of us know what we believe, but are not quite sure how to say it or how to take advantage of opportunities—indeed, make opportunities—to present it. The author brings to bear his own experience, working through his own weaknesses and anxieties as well as the approaches that he has seen to be effective. Combining biblical wisdom with common sense, he knows that personal evangelism is a team sport. It is not something that we do alone, as if we could "close the deal" in every encounter. Furthermore, he knows that the goal of personal evangelism according to our Lord and his apostles is not adding a notch to our belt but adding neighbors to the church.

We are understandably wary of programs that promise to revolutionize the world and trigger mass conversions. This is not that kind of book. But if just one reader—perhaps you or I—became more prepared to give to the next person we encounter a reason for the hope that we have, then *Words in Season* will have been worth more than its weight in gold.

ONE

STARTING IN THE RIGHT PLACE: GOD AND HIS GOSPEL

The culture we inhabit in the 21st century is all about choice. From the food we buy to the clothes we wear, to the cars we drive, intelligent, informed decisions are vital to discern the good from the bad, the helpful from the wasteful, the lasting from the disposable.

When it comes to the subject of personal evangelism, those who desire to learn are faced with the same dilemma—the need to choose from among a multitude of methods and approaches. Given the many programs, seminars, websites and books on personal evangelism, it's easy to get lost in this forest of choices. Which one is right for you? How would you know? Would a spiritual-gifts test help to determine the best fit? Is such a test even accurate or helpful? Then there's the approach—passive or active? Should you sit back and wait for others to ask you about your faith? Is that too passive? Or will you take an aggressive role by approaching strangers and your neighbors to talk about Jesus? Is that too active? Is there a middle ground? Whatever course of action you are currently practicing or will eventually choose, the bottom line is, if you are a Christian, you have to talk about Jesus.

Those who read this book know that talking about Jesus Christ and his gospel are hardly a casual conversation. It's not the same as discussing the weather, sports scores or the latest fashions. Confrontation is inevitable. There are truth claims at stake, and truth claims to make—about the exclusivity of Jesus Christ (John 14:6); about recognizing sin and the need for repentance (Mark 1:15); about the necessity of salvation (Galatians 2:16); about a coming judgment (Acts 17:30-31). Any one of these categories alone can ratchet up anxiety levels. It may cost a friendship, ridicule is a good possibility, and you may even be pegged as a religious nut! The question is: how do we go from here—from fear to faith?

One of my dear friends, who would consider himself in the category of the fearful, still ventures out for the sake of the gospel. The pattern for him is the same every time: he breaks into cold sweats, stammers over words, and feels completely inadequate to the task. To top it off, when reflecting on the witnessing encounter, he often wishes he had said things differently. To him the cycle is one of fear and vain effort. Perhaps you've been there yourself.

There are others who consider themselves as gifted for personal evangelism. They readily share their faith, are comfortable talking to strangers (called, "cold-call" personal evangelism), they willingly distribute gospel tracts (small pamphlets with a Christian message), and some may even attempt open-air evangelism (proclaiming the gospel aloud in the marketplace).

This type of Christian may be our icon, bearing qualities we wish to possess. You may know the type; most churches have some members with these abilities. They frequently bring guests to worship services and they consistently share their testimony about one personal evangelism encounter after another. You listen and watch, in hope that some day you might do the same. Or you may despair of ever attaining to that level. You wish the fear would go away. Discouragement weighs you down. You are weary of the pressure others place on you to share your faith. Quite frankly, it might seem easier to simply wave the white flag, surrendering to fear, and move on. Yet since you've come this far; you know that's not the answer. You just want help.

My hope is that this book will provide the help you desire and a path to the answers you're seeking. If, after reading it, you are more equipped to use the gifts the Lord has given you to share the gospel of Jesus Christ—ridding yourself of the burden of being the next Billy Graham or George Whitefield—the goal will be accomplished. Although you may not know it now, *it is a joy to share the gospel*. You may be fearful while you're doing it, rejection and insults may be your reward, but with the right mindset, you can leave many witnessing encounters rejoicing! And remember, through us, broken

25

vessels that we are, God the Holy Spirit chooses to call his own to himself (Acts 16:11-15). This in itself is a cause for great encouragement. So where do we begin?

The Attributes of God

In many Sunday school classes, children are taught that God is big! A teacher stands before her students and stretches her arms out as wide as she can to demonstrate the grandeur of God. The children get it, and so do we. God is big, but perhaps bigger than we realize. As the Westminster Catechism teaches, "God is a Spirit, infinite, eternal, and unchangeable, in his being, wisdom, power, holiness, justice, goodness, and truth." We can spend pages mining the depths of just one of those attributes.

Take, for example, God's eternality. The psalmist writes, "Before the mountains were brought forth, or ever you had formed the earth and the world, from everlasting to everlasting you are God" (Psalm 90:2). It is easy to read over this verse and say, "Yes, I get it," but do we, really? "Eternality" is a category that we use to express our understanding that God always was. "Before the mountains were brought forth," the psalmist says. Let us take that a step further. "Before *time* was brought forth."

God transcends time and space. To think outside of these categories is impossible. When someone says, for example, the words, "pink elephant," what comes to mind? Now think about "black." What do you see? Next, picture in your mind what "nothing" looks like. Can you picture it? Since we have never seen "nothing," the best our minds can likely do is to see it as "black"— a dark space. But even as you attempt to picture "nothing," you're still doing it in terms of time and space. *Yet God transcends those categories.*

How then shall we attempt to understand God's eternality? By recognizing that our understanding is limited. We can struggle with the concept, but at the end of the day it comes down to trusting that God is who he says he is, because we believe that his word is reliable (1 Timothy 3:16-17; 2 Peter 1:16-21). We know that God is eternal. The difficulty is in expressing what that means in limited human terms. Nevertheless, along with the psalmist, we confess: you, O Lord, are "from everlasting to everlasting," and you "are enthroned forever" (Psalm 90:2; 102:12). Or with the Sunday school teacher, we can simply say, "God is big!"

What about God's holiness? (Isaiah 57:15; John 17:11; Revelation 4:8.) This is another attribute that should give us pause. Sadly, however, because the word is used casually today in exclamatory phrases such as "holy cow!" or "holy smoke!" it has lost its power and impact. Yet when the prophet Isaiah is confronted with the vision of a *holy* God, he is driven trembling to his knees.

"For in the year King Uzziah died," Isaiah writes in chapter 6, "I saw the Lord sitting upon a throne, high and lifted up; and the train of his robe filled the temple. Above him stood the seraphim...and one called to another and said: "Holy, holy, holy is the Lord of hosts; the whole earth is full of his glory!"" (Isaiah 6:1-3).

While portions of Bible stories have been made into movies, no producer has attempted to capture this scene. No movie can fully grasp the splendor here revealed. Mere words are not enough. Our expectation as Christians is that that we will experience this glory one day, when we are ushered into the presence of God (Revelation 21:1-4). Until that day comes, we are left with a glimpse through the pages of scripture.

There are numerous references to the holiness of God in the Bible. The question is, "What does holiness mean?" Very briefly, it means that God is completely set apart and committed to all that he does. Isaiah's vision portrays this by what he says and by what he does not say. Sometimes what is not said is just as significant as what is said. Consider the following illustration.

When I was a child, my mother took me to Las Vegas, Nevada to see Siegfried and Roy, a popular magic show. I was amazed by what I saw—the flashing lights, the animals, the loud noises, and the mirrors. Our seats were at the edge of the stage. Siegfried and Roy made people float in the air, others completely disappeared, and wild tigers obeyed their every command. Looking back, I realized the method to this spectacular madness. I was so focused on the loud sounds, the flashes, and the myriad of activities taking place on stage that I did not pay attention to the smaller details, details that may have given me insight into their magic tricks. To figure them out, of course, would have been no fun at all. My mother did not take me to the magic show to analyze it but to be amazed.

Isaiah's vision was no magic show. What he saw and described was the grandeur of the Lord. And though we are amazed by what he wrote, some things were left unwritten. This is important to help us gain greater insight into Isaiah's vision and the *holiness* of God.

Continue reading verses 4-8 of Isaiah's vision. Other than in verse 1, King Uzziah's name is no longer mentioned. This is significant. In Isaiah's day, the king played an important role. Yet in the presence of God, just as when the moon is covered by the

28

sun, Uzziah's kingship was eclipsed. Why? Because "my eyes have seen the King, the Lord of hosts!" (Isaiah 6:5). For "who is like the Lord our God, who is seated on high, who looks far down on the heavens and the earth?" (Psalm 113:5-6). The answer is, "No one!"

Uzziah's kingship, though valuable, did not remotely compare to the Lord's, the King of all Creation. Is there a human whose glory fills the entire earth (Isaiah 6:3)? While Uzziah experienced a degree of glory, it was limited to the area where he exercised his authority. Is there someone with myriads upon myriads of angelic hosts (armies) at his bidding, willing to go to war on command (Isaiah 6:3)? As a king, Uzziah had soldiers at his disposal who were prepared for war but not like the innumerable angels at God's command. Nor was Uzziah's kingdom of any significant consequence, representing as it did just a small portion of the world at that time. Yet God's kingship covers the earth, the universe, and heaven itself (Isaiah 6:1-4).

Being confronted with what Isaiah was shown, how would we respond? Likely, as Isaiah did—with amazement, wonder, and fear (Isaiah 6:5). While such visions are limited to the prophetic office, Isaiah noticed, as we should, that God is *holy*. He is set apart. He reigns over heaven and earth, a task that even King Uzziah was not designated to do. He is committed to all that he does, which includes his sovereign control over the nations. There is no flaw or deviation within him. All that he does is good and right.

In contrast, King Uzziah's commitment to what is good and right was half-hearted and flawed. In 2 Chronicles 26 it says that Uzziah's heart became divided as he grew strong and proud, the end of which was his destruction (2 Chronicles 26:16). If holiness

29

means absolute commitment (no deviation or double-mindedness), as well as being set apart, the only one who is able to fit such a description is the Lord of Armies. (Notice in Exodus 3:5, God states that the ground is *holy*. What does he mean but that the ground is set apart and committed for a certain function?).

Another attribute of God is his righteousness. Righteousness is associated with making proper judgments (Genesis 18:25; Psalm 97:2). Knowing that God does this perfectly, our thoughts may turn to consider an earthly example by way of comparison. Let's look at human judges and the justice system. We know from what we see and read that no earthly judge exudes the righteousness that is in God. Indeed, "To whom shall we compare him? Or who is his equal?" (Isaiah 40:25). For that reason, this example falls clearly short; nevertheless, for the sake of making a point, let's pursue it.

In America alone, hundreds of court cases occur every day. Laws are broken, charges are laid, and people appear before judges. Cases are presented, deliberations made and judgments are rendered. The expectation is that proper judgments are rendered and justice is satisfied. Another expectation is that the judgment is not arbitrary but is based on a standard—the laws of the land.

In a similar fashion, God executes judgments. Since all that he does is good and right, he cannot make a bad decision. It would be both against his nature and against the laws and rules that he himself made. But the rules that he follows are not externally imposed upon him as they are with earthly judges, since the rules and laws derive from who he is. The prophet Daniel, in reflecting upon God, said, "…the Lord our God is righteous in all the works that he has done…" (Daniel 9:14). Similarly, the prophet Jeremiah said, "Righteous are you, O Lord" (Jeremiah 12:1).

God is also just, infinite, and good. In his personhood, he is triune. He exists in three persons, yet he is one God (Isaiah 40:3; Matthew 28:19; Mark 1:3; John 1:1-3; 5:18; 20:28; Acts 5:3, et. al.).

We could devote volumes to considering the attributes of God. Thankfully, many books have already been written, some with large sections dedicated to this area of theology (*Pilgrim Theology: Core Doctrines for Christian Disciples* by Michael Horton is one good example). Consider taking time to study and be overwhelmed by the attributes of God and his personhood.

The Drama

Many of us enjoy a good drama. Done well, dramas have a way of captivating our complete attention. Whether in book form or on the screen, as the nail-biting events unfold, we wonder what will happen next.

What better drama is there than the unfolding mystery of the Bible? According to one Christian author, the Bible has it all. It involves truth, mystery, deception, and an unimaginable climax. Who would not want to know this story? Or better yet, who would not want to participate *in this story*? What makes the Bible a unique form of drama is that we are not simply watching it unfold. Each one of us is an actor in the story. This is reality television at its best.

Consider the beginning. Although God existed before he created space and time, when he did create it, he entered into his own creation. He began with nothing only later to create light (Genesis 1:3). He separated the light from the darkness calling the light, "Day," and the darkness, "Night" (Genesis 1: 5). He divided land from sky and water, filling the sky with birds, the seas with fish and the land with creatures (Genesis 1:6-8, 11-25). The rhythm of the days was established—evening and morning. From Day One to Day Six, he created. The climax of creation approached. What would God do now? "Then God said, "Let us make man in our image, after our likeness"" (Genesis 1:26). In the midst of his creation, he made a space for us. He created mankind, both male and female, in his image and after his likeness. Mankind would resemble God in certain ways (Ephesians 4:24). As God is holy, man was to be holy. As God is righteous, man was to be righteous.

As well as resembling God in certain inner qualities, man was also created to act in a God-like manner. Just as God had dominion over all that he created, Adam and his wife were given dominion over the birds of the air, the fish of the sea, and creatures on the land. Just as God, the King of the universe, named the light, "Day," the darkness, "Night," and the expanse, "Heaven," so too Adam was granted this same privilege (Genesis 2:19-23). Naming was a royal function that demonstrated kingly authority (Genesis 17:5, 15; 41:45; John 1:42). The animals were brought to Adam to name. It was as if he sat upon his earthly throne, his subjects were brought to him, and he gave them a new name. No wonder the Psalmist said, "You have made him a little lower than the heavenly beings and crowned him with glory and honor" (Psalm 8:5). But sadly all of this, in its purity, was lost.

The Fall

Just as the word "holy" has lost some of its impact, so the phrase, "The Fall," has lost its ability to disturb us with its stark reality.

"The Fall" is more than a theological category. It is *THE* seismic event in history and is the cause of all the havoc and disorder that exists today. War, disease, death, divorce, conflict and disobedience find their birth in The Fall.

The story is well known. God granted Adam blessings beyond measure. He was a king, blessed with an honorable and noble wife, had wealth, and the perfect living accommodations. Most importantly, Adam and his wife had unmediated access to God. They could speak to God and fellowship with him without fear of reproach. They knew the Lord intimately. He was their God and they were his people. The world was theirs! God had only one prohibition. Amid the hundreds of things Adam and his wife could do, God required only that they not eat from the "Tree of Knowledge of Good and Evil."

"Now the serpent," we read, "was more crafty than any other beast of the field that the Lord God had made. He said to the woman, "Did God actually say, you shall not eat of any tree in the garden?"" (Genesis 3:1). The Great Deceiver, Satan, took the form of a serpent and questioned the authority of God. How should Adam and his wife have responded? Firstly, they should have denounced Satan's attempt to deceive them. Secondly, they should have removed him from the garden (Genesis 2:15; Numbers 3:10). By doing this, Adam would have imaged God. Instead, Adam stood by and allowed his wife to be deceived. Once deceived, he followed in her in disobedience (Genesis 3:6).

The freedoms that Adam and his wife enjoyed were now revoked. Once delighting in the presence of God, they now hid from him. Once experiencing complete transparency and trust with each other, they now knew shame and guilt. Adam as head was ultimately responsible. Highlighting the severity of Adam's disobedience, one theologian described it in this way: "Though at first glance it seems to be a small offence, yet, if we look more wistfully [that is, earnestly] upon the matter it will appear to be an exceeding great offence; for thereby intolerable injury was done unto God; as, first, his dominion and authority in his holy command was violated. Secondly, his justice, truth, and power, in his most righteous threatenings, were despised. Thirdly, his most pure and perfect image, wherein man was created in righteousness and true holiness, was utterly defaced. Fourthly, his glory, which, by an active service, the creature should have brought to him, was lost and despoiled."[1]

---

[1] Edward Fisher, Fisher, *The Marrow of Modern Divinity* (Scotland: Christian Focus Publications, 2009), 57.

"By Adam's fall, we sinned, all." As the first man of the human race, Adam represented all of us (Romans 5:12). His sin is our sin. Adam's sin was imputed to us, and even from birth, our nature is bent toward sin (Psalm 51:5; Ephesians 2:1). We are born with a disposition that is against God. Our perfect holiness and righteousness is gone (Jeremiah 17:9; Colossians 1:21). Though before The Fall a perfect image-bearer of God, we now bear the sinful image of man (Genesis 5:3). If ever there is a reason for great and overwhelming sorrow, this is it.

"But God!" These are perhaps two of the most glorious words in the Bible. God did not leave us in our misery and isolation. God intervened in a way that we neither expected nor deserved. He did not leave Adam and his wife—or us—to rot in sin. Instead, God began his great work of redemption.

Redemption

After The Fall, God announced his verdict of judgment. He multiplied the pain of childbearing and announced inevitable familial conflict (Genesis 3:15-16). For Adam, with the ground cursed, work would become tough. "In pain you shall eat of it all the days of your life" (Genesis 3:17). Death was the ultimate penalty for sin (Genesis 3:19).

If the unfolding drama ended here, there would be no hope. God, however, rich in mercy, did not leave humanity in its sin. He made a promise described for us in Genesis 3:15. "I will put enmity between you and the

35

woman, and between your offspring and her offspring; he shall bruise your head, and you shall bruise his heel." Although The Fall created one tribe of people—sons of Satan—God promised that he would intervene and create another tribe of people—sons of God. This new tribe of people would emerge, ultimately, when *he* bruised Satan's head. Adam understood this as good news. That is why he renamed his wife.

Until this point in the drama, Adam's spouse was named, "Wife." It was not until God promised to create a new tribe of people—sons of God—that Adam called his wife's name, Eve (Genesis 3:20). Eve, in the Greek translation of the Old Testament, means *life*. Or as our English translations state, "the mother of all living." Adam heard a promise of *new life*. Though their sin was very great, God would cast their sin, and the penalty of their sin, as far as the East is from the West. Their sin was removed. God not only took something away—their sin—but he also gave them something—Christ's righteousness, pictured when God clothed them with garments of animal skin (Genesis 3:21; 2 Corinthians 5:21).

Just as God killed an animal in the garden, shed its blood, and covered his people with animal skins, so he would later crush his Son and shed his blood to cover sinners with his righteousness and remove their sins (Isaiah 53:1-10; 2 Corinthians 5:21). Adam brought sin and death into the world; the Second Adam, the Son of God incarnate in Jesus Christ, brought righteousness and life (Romans 5:12-21). Life and righteousness are given to all who believe. All of our sins are fully forgiven. Though deserving of God's wrath and curse, Christ took that punishment. Our sin and guilt were transferred to Christ, and his righteousness was credited to us. We now stand perfectly righteous before the Father. He is our God and we are his people. "If anyone is in Christ, he is a new creation" (2 Corinthians 5:17).

Christ's birth, perfect life, sacrificial death, resurrection, and ascension, leads to everlasting life for all of God's people. The debt owed due to sin was nailed to the cross. Paul says God forgave "us all our trespasses, by canceling the record of debt that stood against us with its legal demands. This he set aside, nailing it to the cross" (Colossians 2:13-14). There is no longer enmity between God and us—his people—because Satan's head was bruised. We are now part of another tribe of people—sons of God. In Christ, this is who we are. Do not doubt! Only believe! Christ is ours and we are his. By faith in Christ, this is our guarantee!

We are also guaranteed that the Holy Spirit will steadily transform us into the image of Christ (Romans 12:1-2; Colossians 3:10). Our very minds—that is the way we think—are being shaped to more fully think as Christ thinks. We are being changed so that we can put to death what is earthly in us and live to righteousness. This is our promise until the Lord takes us home. Then we will be like him, and all that he set out to do will be fully realized.

Conclusion

Why begin a book on personal evangelism in this way? You may have concerns about your ability to answer common objections to Christianity. Maybe you are concerned about clearly articulating the good news of Jesus Christ. You may wonder if you have the gifts to share your faith. Many of these concerns will be addressed, but what we need to do is start where it matters most—with God and his gospel!

Life begins with God, not man. When we place our desires above what God requires, the results are already in (read Genesis 3 again). When God is the focus, giving him all the glory and honor that is due his name, only then can we rightly conduct ourselves. This is true in all areas of life, personal evangelism included. Without God's initiating love and grace in Jesus, there is no good news to share. Without God's mercy and compassion, we would be blind to the truths of the gospel. Without God's sympathy and condescension, the penalty for our sins would remain. But with all of the above, and more, we have great news to believe and share.

Question: "What is your only comfort in life and death?" The Heidelberg Catechism gives an answer that we should carry with us throughout our lives: "That I with body and soul, both in life and death, am not my own, but belong to my faithful Savior Jesus Christ; who, with his precious blood, has satisfied for all my sins, and delivered me from all the power of the devil; and so preserves me that without the will of my heavenly Father, not a hair can fall from my head; yea, that all things must be subservient to my salvation, and therefore, by his Holy Spirit, he also assures me of eternal life, and makes me sincerely willing and ready, henceforth, to live unto him."

Discussion Questions

1. When discussing personal evangelism, there are many places we can start. Why start with God and his gospel?

2. How did Adam disobey God in the garden? How has this affected you?

3. Did Adam hear good news in the garden? How do you know?

4. Based on the information in this chapter and your personal knowledge of the Bible, what is the good news of Jesus Christ?

5. What are the benefits of the good news? Are these benefits applied to you? How do you know?

6. Are you willing to commit Heidelberg Catechism question and answer number one to memory? If so, hold yourself accountable and set a date.

TWO

THE CHURCH: A GREAT ANNOUNCEMENT AND A GREAT COMMISSION

In 1995 pop artist Michael Jackson released a song titled, "You Are Not Alone." In the opening stanza of this love song, Jackson sings, "Another day has gone, I'm still all alone. How could this be?" Although the remainder of the song answers that question, Jackson's song fits into a greater love story—finding, having, and keeping a significant other.

Christians are involved in the ultimate love story. "For God so loved the world..." we read in John 3:16, "that he gave his only begotten Son, that whosoever should believe in him shall not perish but have everlasting life." Later, the apostle Paul, by the inspiration of the Spirit, described Christ as the bridegroom and the Church as the bride (Ephesians 5:32). There is a special level of intimacy that Christ has with his Church, which, as in a marriage, is only experienced by those in the relationship. *Indeed, this is love!*

The unfolding drama from Genesis to Revelation is the greatest love story of all time. God's initiating love shed abroad in our hearts, because of the person and work of the Lord Jesus Christ, is beyond comparison to any love song or story that has or might yet be written. The Son of God came to this earth to capture *a people*, his Church, with his love, by living, dying, and rising from the grave. Christ died *for a people*. We are not spiritual nomads, even though we may think that way sometimes—that we are all alone. The Bible clearly states that we are baptized into one body, the Church, *as his people* (1 Corinthians 12:13). Christ did not save us to walk the earth alone; he saved us as pilgrims who gather to receive his gifts and execute his laws. Both his gifts and his laws are presented in the Church's Great Announcement and the Church's Great Commission.

The Church's Mission

After the resurrection of Jesus, the disciples met with him on a mountain. There they worshiped him and received what our Bible translations call, "The Great Commission." To many Christians, the main emphasis in this Commission is found in the word "Go!" But before this pronouncement of Christ, he makes an announcement—a Great Announcement. Jesus says, "All authority in heaven and on earth has been given to me"

(Matthew 28:18). Before anyone is commanded to "Go!" Jesus informs his disciples what will give them the power and motivation *to go*. It had nothing to do with their natural abilities. It was not how persuasive or eloquent they could be. Rather, it was about what Jesus had done by conquering sin, Satan, and death once and for all (Matthew 28:6). He accomplished all that his Father gave him to do (John 17:4). He is the firstborn from the dead (Colossians 1:18). He is the King and Judge of all the living (John 5:22). He is the Christ, the Son, now incarnate, as king, for his people (Mark 8:29).

All this is likely familiar—Doctrine 101. But consider this: not only is Jesus truly God—he is also truly man. Therefore making such claims as the *God-man* is something new. Never before has a *man* spoken with such authority, especially one who has recently risen from the dead—not King David, not the prophet Elijah, not John the Baptist. But now the greater King, the able Prophet, and the one to whom John the Baptist pointed, has returned from the grave as the God-man, and *he has been given all authority in heaven and on earth*. He is King Jesus, the sinless, perfect, spotless Lamb of God who came to take away the sin of the world (John 1:29). The Church does not exist apart from the person and work of the Lord Jesus Christ. Without Christ fulfilling his mission, we would have no mission (Psalm 110). But because of what Christ has done, his people can "Go!" into all the nations and make disciples by baptizing and teaching. This is the mission of the Church, a Great

Commission based on a Great Announcement. The book of Acts reflects this unfolding.

Acts

Shortly after Jesus' Commission to his disciples in Matthew 28:18-20, he gave them a promise in Acts 1:8: "But you will receive power when the Holy Spirit has come upon you, and you will be my witnesses in Jerusalem and in all Judea and Samaria, and to the end of the earth."

The first stage of the Acts 1:8 promise is fulfilled soon after in Jerusalem when over 3000 souls turn to the Lord and are baptized after hearing the gospel through Peter's preaching (Acts 2:41). Those same souls later "devoted themselves to the apostles' teaching and the fellowship, to the breaking of bread and the prayers" (Acts 2:42). The work did not end here, however. The gospel still needed to reach Judea, Samaria, and the ends of the earth.

In Acts 8, Philip went to Samaria preaching the word of God. Many believed in Jesus and were baptized (Acts 8:12). Yet, to fulfill the command given to the apostles (Acts 1:8), other apostles went to Samaria to be witnesses to the word of God spreading in that region. As Luke writes, "Now when the apostles at Jerusalem heard that Samaria had received the word of God, they sent to them Peter and John" (Acts 8:14). The gospel continued to spread. With power and authority, the word of God reached Judea (Acts 8:1), the Gentiles (Acts 10), and the ends of the known world (Acts 13-28). As you read this, consider how far the gospel has spread. *It has even come to you.* The Great Commission, based on a Great Announcement, has penetrated ethnic, cultural, and international boundaries so that you would hear about Jesus Christ's life, death, resurrection, and ascension and turn to him in repentance and faith being baptized in the name of the Triune God. Now, having been added to the Church, which is essential in every Christian's life, you are able to participate in the Great Commission in two ways.

You Are a Recipient

Sermons on the Great Commission, in my experience, suggest that the Commission is only something that affects *others* (i.e., unbelievers). In other words, Christians are the ones who carry out the Great Commission and unbelievers are the recipients. Over the years, however, I have come to a different conclusion.

Every Lord's Day believers listen to the good news of Jesus Christ in their local churches. They come to worship recognizing that over the past week they have sinned against God in thought, word, and deed. Faithful Christians recognize that in and of themselves, they cannot stand before a holy and righteous God. While the world may tempt us to believe that we can be good enough to merit God's favor, we know the lie when we hear it, although the notion may be hard to resist. An honest assessment is that we deserve God's wrath and curse. Yet the minister stands before God's people and speaks words of grace. He says that while we are not good enough, there is one who is—Jesus—and in him we are righteous before God.

Some 2000 years ago, the second person of the Godhead took on flesh (John 1:14). He was perfect in thought, word, and deed (Hebrews 4:15). While everyone lobbed false accusations at him, he loved as only the perfect God-man could (1 Peter 2:23). Jesus was holy and righteous. Although he deserved no punishment, he voluntarily took up the cross to bear the sins of his people (Matthew 1:21). The apostle Paul said, "For our sake he made him to be sin who knew no sin, so that in him we might become the righteousness of God" (2 Corinthians 5:21). The apostle Peter said, "He himself bore our sins in his body on the tree…by his wounds you have been healed" (1 Peter 2:24). And now there is therefore "no condemnation for those who are in Christ Jesus" (Romans 8: 1).

This is what Christians wait to hear and *receive* at the beginning of each week—the good news of Jesus Christ. "For by grace you have been saved through faith. And this is not your own doing; it is the gift of God, not as a result of works, so that no one may boast" (Ephesians 2:8-9). By God's grace and the work of the Holy Spirit, faith is strengthened by the preaching of the scriptures and, as frequently as your church observes, the administration of baptism and the Lord's Supper. In light of this good news, one can respond by offering God the praise that is due him alone and live a life worthy of the calling of the gospel (Romans 12:1-2; Ephesians 4:1).

This makes us as God's people recipients of the Great Commission. Initiated as disciples by baptism in the name of the Father and of the Son and of the Holy Spirit, we continue to be taught all that the Lord has commanded (Matthew 28:19-20). He also assures us that he is with us, always, even to the end of the age.

As recipients of the Great Commission (or disciples of Christ), we are equipped over a lifetime; it is not a brand (the term, "disciple") placed upon us in our baptism never to be considered again. Rather, it is a name that displays our allegiance, a commitment to learning, to growing, and discipleship throughout our lives (Matthew 28:20). But Christians are not only recipients, we are also contributors.

You Are a Contributor

I spent ten years in the United States Navy. It was a time of adventure, learning, and growing. One aspect of the military I particularly enjoyed was the promotion system. A good quarterly evaluation and a high score on the rating exam normally led to a promotion. It meant higher pay and increased responsibility.

My first promotion was to workstation supervisor (a fancy word for "boss"). I was both excited and scared. People were now working under me, and I was responsible for their well-being. Improper training meant a workstation penalty. If I did not counsel them correctly about personal matters, it showed. My supervisor placed a lot of pressure on me. I struggled with confusion and uncertainty. Nevertheless, because of my promotion, I needed to rise to a new level of competency.

The Great Commission is similar. In Christ, we are given new life. We are united to Christ and have the forgiveness of sins and perfect righteousness—justification. We are being sanctified and promised eternal life. All the promises are yes and amen in the Son (2 Corinthians 1:20). So what do we do now?

As followers of Christ, commissioned by the Father and equipped by the Holy Spirit, how do we obey the Great Commission? Do we simply start talking about Jesus? How do we, as disciples, teach people all that Jesus commanded? Should all Christians baptize, even those not ordained? What is our role in this new position, a disciple of Jesus Christ? Many Christians wrestle with these questions.

In Matthew 28 Jesus is speaking to his eleven disciples (later called "apostles") who were given a unique position during a special time. They were to teach the whole counsel of God and to administer the sacraments (Acts 1:21-22; 1 Corinthians 3:11; 2 Peter 1:16). With the passing of the apostles, God equipped his Church for leadership by calling pastors to lead in the ministry of both word and sacraments (1 Timothy 3:1-7; 5:17; 2 Timothy 4:1-5). Ministers are called to "preach the word; to be ready in season and out of season; to reprove, rebuke, and exhort, with complete patience and teaching…to always be sober-minded, endure suffering, do the work of an evangelist, fulfill your ministry" (2 Timothy 4:2, 5). For those who are not ordained pastors, this may not help much. Do not fear! John Dickson puts it well when he writes:

> [W]hile Matthew would have thought the specifics refer directly to the "eleven disciples" and those entrusted with the apostolic mission afterward (teachers, evangelists, etc.), the broad thrust of the Lord's command applies to all who know him. We might not all "go" throughout the nations, "teach" everything Jesus commanded and "baptize," but we do all promote the gospel—through our prayers, good works, public praise, financial support of gospel workers and daily conversations—and so contribute to making disciples of all nations. We all share in the aptly called Great Commission.[2]

Every believer in the Lord Jesus Christ is filled with the Spirit of the living God and has the empowerment to "proclaim the excellencies of him who called you out of darkness into his marvelous light" (1 Peter 2:9). Yes, every believer!

---

[2] John Dickson, *The Best Kept Secret of Christian Mission: Promoting the Gospel with More Than Our Lips* (Zondervan: Grand Rapids, 2010), 34.

We see evidence of this throughout the Gospels and the Pauline epistles. Jesus sent out more than just twelve (Luke 10:1-12). Paul encouraged the entire church at Corinth to imitate him as he sought the salvation of all (1 Corinthians 10:31-11:1). There were laypeople who were already actively engaged in personal evangelism before Paul wrote to the Church at Philippi (Philippians 1:12-18a). Paul told the Church at Colossae to "walk in wisdom toward outsiders, making the best use of the time. Let your speech always be gracious, seasoned with salt, so that you may know how you ought to answer each person" (Colossians 4:5-6). The cumulative evidence suggests that we are all called to be witnesses of God's mighty acts. As one pastor put it, "Witnesses are not mute." And when we are given the privilege to speak about the glories of God in Christ, what a blessing it is to know Christ said, "I am with you always, to the end of the age" (Matthew 28:20).

The Church's Witness

As we will see later in more depth, God's word is clear about our individual responsibility to share the gospel. In time, sharing the gospel and inviting others to church will become a great joy. In the meantime, keep in mind that the Church has the responsibility to witness. That comes as she testifies of the Lord Jesus Christ, through the preaching of the word and the administration of the sacraments. The marks of the Church include the preaching of the holy gospel and the administration of the sacraments (a third mark is faithful discipline). Without these marks, a church is unfaithful.

By inviting others to church, they will be effectively witnessed to (i.e., evangelism occurs) as the word of God is faithfully preached and the sacraments, in tangible and visible form, testify to the person and work of the Lord Jesus Christ.

As the scriptures are proclaimed, the Holy Spirit pricks the consciences of unbelievers convicting them of sin, righteousness, and judgment (John 16:8). As the law of God thunders from the pulpit, as the Spirit awakens an unbeliever's conscience, he will conclude that he is without hope. Despite what the world preaches, God doesn't grade on a curve. God's standard for acceptance is perfection! Since no mere human meets that standard, our only hope is that God provide another way for reconciliation with himself.

With hearts humbled and softened by the law, the good news of Jesus Christ is well received. It provides the hope and acceptance for which all long. The gospel helps us—and unbelievers—better understand the depths that God underwent in order to claim a people for himself. In Christ, he is our God and we are his people. Though at one time we were afar off, God brought us near by the blood of Christ (Ephesians 2:15-17).

Baptism also testifies to Christ and his work. Unfortunately, however, baptism is sometimes viewed as a spectator sport. In other words, the only person affected by baptism is the one receiving the sacrament. But that's not true! While believers are built up in their faith as they observe baptism, this sacrament says a lot to unbelievers as well.

The Westminster Larger Catechism Q/A 165 says, "Baptism is a sacrament of the New Testament, wherein Christ hath ordained the washing with water in the name of the Father, and of the Son, and of the Holy Ghost, to be a sign and seal of ingrafting into himself, of remission of sins by his blood, and regeneration by his Spirit; of adoption, and resurrection unto everlasting life; and whereby the parties baptized are solemnly admitted into the visible church, and enter into an open and professed engagement to be wholly and only the Lord's."

By faith in Christ, all of these blessings belong to the party baptized—not so for unbelievers. They remain in their sin, are under God's wrath and curse, and still belong wholly to the world. In fact, their god is the Devil and Christ is their judge (John 5:27; Ephesians 2:1-3). The washing away of sin and adoption into the household of God, as symbolized in baptism, does not belong to them. They are separated from the visible church and at war with God. Yet, if they repent of their sins and turn to Christ in faith alone, they will receive all the blessings signified in baptism.

The Lord's Supper is also an effective witness. Although seemingly insignificant—a small piece of bread and a quarter of an ounce of wine (or juice)—it roars of judgment, but also grace, for unbelievers. The Lion of Judah, though slain, lives. He is seated at the right hand of God the Father almighty, and as the Apostles' Creed says, "from there he will come to judge the living and the dead."

What provides the basis for this confession? The apostle Paul writes, "For as often as you eat this bread and drink this cup, you proclaim the Lord's death until he comes again" (1 Corinthians 11:26). Jesus is alive and shall return to claim his Church. He will also judge all outsiders, those outside of union with Christ. They are awaiting judgment. The Lord's Supper testifies!

Communion also announces what is required to retire God's wrath and step into his grace. ""This is my body which is for you. Do this in remembrance of me." In the same way he also took the cup, after supper, saying, "This cup is the new covenant in my blood. Do this, as often as you drink it, in remembrance of me"" (1 Corinthians 11:24-25). Jesus' body must be broken and his blood must be shed at the hands of lawless men (Acts 2:23). He needed to be stripped of his clothes, thorns placed on his head, mocked, struck, and crucified as his Father's fury was unleashed on him for the sins of his people (Matthew 27:27-31). All this, and more, Communion says to unbelievers as the words of institution are spoken and the bread and cup passed.

The word of God preached and the two sacraments instituted by Jesus in the New Testament provide a clear delineation between Christians and outsiders. They are an effective witness to an unbelieving world (Westminster Larger Catechism Q/A 154, 162). And by the grace of God that is distributed therein, they bid unbelievers,

"Come!" "Come to me, all who labor and are heavy laden, and I will give you rest. Take my yoke upon you, and learn from me, for I am gentle and lowly in heart, and you will find rest for your souls. For my yoke is easy, and my burden is light" (Matthew 11:28-30).

Conclusion

Christians take part in the Church's mission as both recipients and contributors. As recipients, God's people receive his good gifts in the preaching of the word and the administration of the sacraments. Our assurance is that "we do not have a high priest who is unable to sympathize with our weaknesses, but one who in every respect has been tempted as we are, yet without sin" (Hebrews 4:15). This one Jesus, "by a single offering...has perfected for all time those who are being sanctified" (Hebrews 10:14). "For," as Paul says, "I am sure that neither death nor life, nor angels nor rulers, nor things present nor things to come, nor powers, nor height nor depth, nor anything else in all creation, will be able to separate us from the love of God in Christ Jesus our Lord" (Romans 8:38-39).

Christians also contribute to the Great Commission. Pastors preach the gospel and administer the sacraments thereby making disciples. Laypersons and office-bearers alike "promote the gospel—through our prayers, good works, public praise, financial support of gospel workers and daily conversations—and so contribute to making disciples of all nations." It is a daunting task, but one that is wholly beneficial as multitudes of people "from every tribe and language and people and nation" move from darkness to light and from death to life by the grace and goodness of our precious Savior, Jesus Christ (Revelation 5:9). Are you involved in this Great Commission? You should be, if you bear the name of Christ.

Discussion Questions

1. On what, or on whom, is the Church's mission based? Use Scripture to support your answer.

2. What is the Church's mission? How is it executed in the book of Acts?

3. Are you a recipient of the Church's mission? How so? How frequently?

4. Are you a contributor to the Church's mission? Base your answer on some of the scripture citations used in this chapter.

5. How is the Church a witness? Does that bring you confidence if you invite people to church?

THREE

INDIVIDUAL RESPONSIBILITY: A FEARFUL EXPECTATION

Billy Graham is said to have reached over two billion people during his 58 years of public ministry. He traveled to at least six continents and visited more than 20 countries. Reportedly, millions came to know the name of Jesus Christ through his itinerant preaching. While Billy Graham is perhaps the most famous evangelist during the 20th century, in the 18th century some suggest it was George Whitefield. While his numbers may not be as lofty, he was known as an amazing evangelist. Whitefield traveled throughout the New England colonies preaching Christ. Meeting in the open fields, thousands heard the call to repentance and faith.

Whitefield and Graham are two examples of famous evangelists. Many hold them up as standard bearers. Some desire to emulate their ministry—that is, our evangelist forefathers' boldness, eloquence and zeal. After all, the call is, "You will be my witnesses in

Jerusalem and in all Judea and Samaria, and to the end of the earth." So the question is, what are you waiting for? Bury your fears, get over your anxiety, and start talking to others about Jesus Christ. Why wait? There's no time like the present!

Perhaps you've heard something like this. Maybe you've felt pressure to be the next Billy Graham or George Whitefield. Staying in your neighborhood and in your vocation might not seem good enough. You must be a missionary. There are unreached people locally and abroad waiting for your ministry. But think about it: Are all Christians meant to be evangelists and missionaries (Ephesians 4:11)? Where do gifts fit into the equation?

The pressure of others may turn you off and push you away from evangelistic responsibility. Or quite possibly you shudder at the thought of talking to others about Christ. A Gallup poll reports that 40% of U.S. respondents fear public speaking, and you consider yourself to be among the 40%. The only thing that frightens Americans more was ophidiophobia (a fear of snakes).[3]

For some, the thought of witnessing leads to clammy hands, weak knees, a cracked voice, and a mind that turns to mush when opportunities are available to share the gospel. So how fair is it for you to be compared to one of the great evangelists?

---

[3] http://www.gallup.com/poll/1891/Snakes-Top-List-Americans-Fears.aspx

If God has not called you to be a missionary, do not feel obligated to become something you are not meant to be. This insight was revolutionary for me, but from the opposite end. I was the guy who pressured everyone I knew to become zealous evangelists. Instead of telling them to be like George Whitefield or Billy Graham, however, I wanted them to be like me! If they were not sharing the gospel with their unsaved families members, neighbors, and strangers with the same frequency as me, something was wrong with them.

My arrogance pushed people away. People later said they tried to avoid me. I was zealous, but unwise. Instead of bringing people along by encouraging the gifts in them, I tried to remake them in my image. Thankfully in God's grace we grow, learn, and move on. But perhaps those whom we have affected have not moved on. They may still be concerned about their gifts in this area. Does this describe you?

Or when confronted with the opportunity to share the gospel, do you wonder: "What will they say?" or "How will they respond?" You may be concerned about pushing your friends and neighbors away. Or you may not feel adequately prepared. "What if I say something wrong?" Fear begins to overtake the desire to share Christ crucified.

We bring much baggage to the table, and baggage requires some unloading and unpacking. So let's begin the job by considering some obstacles to be removed or altered as we contemplate sharing the gospel.

Stage Fright

One afternoon in Escondido, California, I decided to eat at a local restaurant. Leaving my truck, I noticed a gospel tract in the compartment on the driver's door. Placing it in my pocket, I decided to give it away before getting back into my truck. I made it to the restaurant and out again without giving away the tract. While walking to my vehicle, a gentleman in a work uniform came by. I decided to give the tract to him. As soon as I pulled it from my pocket, my heart raced and my hands became sweaty. I had yet to open my mouth. Stage fright kicked in. My plan was to give him the gospel tract and leave. But then he asked, "What's this?" My getaway plan failed; I had to give an account of my faith. The Lord blessed the opportunity and this gentleman began attending my church.

It seems that no amount of witnessing removes stage fright, the fear of public speaking. Maybe that is a good thing. Fear can cause us to stop trusting our own abilities. It makes us realize that we cannot do this on our own. We need the strength of Another. Fear can keep us both humble and looking to Christ for strength. Wayne Minnick, professor emeritus at Florida State University, put it this way: "Stage fright is…an appropriate physical and emotional peak for a challenging experience. Stage fright, then, can help you speak with distinction. If you were indifferent, you would undoubtedly do poorly."[4] Fear can be a good thing. Do not let it cripple your witness, but let it cause you to lean on Christ, and in the words of Wayne Minnick, "help you speak with distinction."

I Don't Know What They Will Say

Truth be told, I do not often go to the grocery store with my wife. When I do go, however, I usually stand around or am told what to do. My presence probably adds an hour to the process. It's not that I mind going to the grocery store, but since marrying I stopped going regularly. The few times I do go are like visiting a new city. I don't know where things are, but I go anyway. It makes my wife happy.

One sunny day in Southern California my wife and I were leaving the grocery store. A man was standing nearby requesting donations for a charity. I was both curious about the charity, and also saw an opportunity to talk about Christ. I asked him some basic questions about his organization and he responded well, much like a well-rehearsed car salesman. When he finished, I told him that I was uninterested in contributing to his cause. He was displeased, but I took advantage of the situation anyway. I asked him if I could share some things with him. He said, "Sure."

---

[4] Wayne C. Minnick, *Public Speaking*, 2ed. (Boston: Houghton Mifflin Company, 1983), 63.

He allowed me to talk without interruption. I told him about God as Creator, Judge, and Redeemer. I thought, "This is my kind of witnessing encounter." To my surprise, when I was done, he assented to a few things and began to engage me with some of his knowledge, quoting directly from the Bible. In fact, one of the passages he quoted caught me by surprise. "In my Father's house are many rooms. If it were not so, would I have told you that I go to prepare a place for you? And if I go and prepare a place for you, I will come again and will take you to myself, that where I am you may be also" (John 14:2-3).

This man used John 14:2-3 to claim that, although he was not a Christian, God prepared a place for him in heaven. This caught me by surprise. It wasn't that I didn't have an answer. I knew that unbelievers have no part in heaven. What caught me by surprise was the ease and fluency with which he quoted scripture. It wasn't something I expected, and it felt as if a cat had caught my tongue. I had nothing to say in response.

I stumbled over my words, back-peddled and ever so slightly shuffled around his statement. Thankfully, however, this did not stop me from sharing my faith. Although I went into the conversation not knowing what he would say, and in the midst of our conversation I was not quick-witted enough to answer his objection, I still shared Christ. That man's salvation is not based on the immediacy of my response, but on the Holy Spirit opening his eyes and ears to the gospel of Jesus Christ.

(This does not mean that we remain ignorant to common objections). This man needed to have his sin exposed by the law and his heart comforted by the gospel. He needed to know that in Christ there is no condemnation (Romans 8:1). He needed to be told that Christ is not one way among many, but the only way, the truth, and the life (John 14:6). Despite my inadequacies, the message was placed before him and God will do what he pleases with his word.

I Don't Know Enough

A beautiful characteristic of Christianity is that the word of God is inexhaustible. Familiar passages read over the years can suddenly be seen in a new and fuller light. Perhaps you have experienced this firsthand. These discoveries fuel your desire for greater study of the scriptures.

Some, however, may see this in the opposite light, as something lacking in their own Bible knowledge. But all Christians face this deficiency. Simply because the word is so full, we can never mine all of its contents. So in essence, we are all in the same boat.

Bible knowledge and its application is a life-long journey. For those called to attend seminary, they quickly realize, even after graduation, how much they still need to learn. Regardless of how deep your Bible knowledge extends, consider yourself a disciple that is in constant need of being taught the word of God (Matthew 28:20). Unbelievers may ask questions that you may not be able to answer immediately. There are also mysteries we may never unravel. Instead of allowing this to impede our witness, let it drive us to the scriptures. There is gold to mine on every page.

It is also not a sign of weakness to say, "I don't know." If someone asks a question and you do not know the answer, it's dishonest to bluff your way through. People can generally spot a phony. Instead, the better way is to say you will get back to them later. Just be sure to follow up. This is an honest response, and will allow you to continue the conversation. This break in discussion will also give you time to prepare questions that you may like to ask in response.

I once went to a friend's house to have a conversation with a Jehovah's Witness. The fellow was extremely intelligent. He knew the original Bible languages (Hebrew and Greek), and was versed in how to respond to common objections against his religion. (At that point in my life I was still rather young in the faith.) He constantly referenced the original languages, but that did not deter me from trying to compete with him. The words "I don't know" should have come out of my mouth more than they did.

I Don't Want to Push People Away

One of the realities of the gospel is that it divides (Matthew 10:21-22, 34-39). Just try sharing Christ with an unbelieving family member. For a season, several of my family members would not talk to me because I shared the law and the gospel with them. They despised the law because it confronted them with the reality that they were not good people. Although they maintained the mantra, "I'm a good person, and as long as I do more good than bad, God will be pleased with me," I reminded them that there is no such thing as a *good person* in God's eyes (Romans 3:10-12). God demands perfection. And since "no flesh shall be justified by the works of the law" (Romans 3:20), they were in trouble. This teaching was offensive to them.

The gospel was also offensive. Christ as both God and man was puzzling to them, and the exclusivity of Jesus as the only means of salvation, they found frustrating. Conversation ceased for a time.

Nevertheless, while the gospel divides, our personalities should not be the cause of division. When sharing the truth of Christ with a hostile family member, friend, or neighbor, our tempers can get the best of us. We may say things in anger or frustration. Our body language may be less than warm, and emails can be unduly harsh. When God in his providence provides an opportunity to share the good news and it is rejected, we can feel personally affronted, or we may respond with distaste for the individual or individuals with whom we have invested much time and energy.

For years I prayed for my mother. I also frequently shared the law and the gospel with her, but sadly our interaction often ended in argument. It was not always her fault. At times, I taunted her; I pressed her in areas where pressure was not needed; I even yelled. When this happened, the offense was not that of the gospel, but her son's arrogance and haughtiness. That was not my intention, but I was not self-controlled enough. By my behavior, I often gave her a reason to reject the gospel and to withdraw from me. At the end of the day, while our intent should never be to push people away from the truth of the gospel, we can rest in the words of our Lord: "I am the good shepherd. I know my own and my own know me" (John 10:14). Thankfully, God saved my mother despite myself, and I had the privilege of preaching at her baptism service.

What Will They Think of Me?

The truth is, we care about what people think of us. That's not always a bad thing (Proverbs 22:1). But it can be. Young people particularly are faced with these issues. The pressures to fit in, to wear certain clothes, to do certain things, and hang out with the "in-crowd" can seem too much to resist. Adults face some of the same pressures, being influenced by the surrounding culture and the desire to maintain a certain reputation. Although we may not admit it at times, self-image issues can be consuming. And sharing the gospel, we fear, could alter peoples' otherwise favorable impression of us.

There are many reasons why sharing the gospel could affect our reputation, but the main reason has to do with the "foolishness of the cross" (1 Corinthians 1:25).

Christianity is the only religion that looks to a Savior outside of oneself, which is contrary to our instincts and the message of every other religion. From early on we are taught that our hard work will get us places. The law and the gospel, on the other hand, reveal our sorry state. The law is a mirror that exposes our blemishes. All ugliness is brought to the light, and can neither be hidden nor removed by our own strength or ability.

The gospel comes along and says, "Although it is your work that got you into this mess, someone else has cleaned up your filth." The gospel tells of our inability to save ourselves. It reminds us that we cannot contribute one ounce to our salvation. This message, especially in the context of the, "pull yourself up by your bootstraps" mentality, is absurd. But this is exactly the message, by God's grace and the power of God the Holy Spirit, which saves us from God and ourselves. "For by grace you have been saved through faith. And this is not your own doing; it is the gift of God, not a result of works, so that no one may boast" (Ephesians 2:8-9).

Our entire worldview is shattered in a moment only to be left with two possible responses to the gospel: denial or acceptance. This places people in a corner. They may begin to think you are narrow-minded because you believe that Jesus Christ is the only way to gain acceptance with God (John 14:6). They may think that you are absurd because you acknowledge that your salvation is completely a free gift from the Lord and there is nothing you can add to it. They may call you crazy because you believe an innocent man, God in the flesh, took the punishment that you deserve. These things are ridiculous in the world's eyes, and perhaps as you share these truths with people, they may think of you differently. Yet in the overall scheme of things, what matters most is what God thinks of you.

Ethnicity and Culture

As the old saying goes, "Birds of a feather flock together." It's easier to talk with those who look, act, and dress like us. The same is true of those with whom we work or live near in the community, or with those in our income bracket. But the moment we step outside of these boundaries, we can become uncomfortable. It's the idea of walking in someone's shoes, of knowing something of their background, their culture, their habits, their language. If you are an African-American who was raised in the suburbs with two parents, how well will you mesh with a Caucasian-American who grew up in a single-parent household surrounded by the drug culture? Or perhaps you grew up in a farming community and now have to communicate with someone raised in the city? Where do you find common ground? Perhaps you were raised in a homeschooling culture? How easy or difficult is it to relate to families who raise their children in public schools?

It begins with attitude. Start by considering cultural and ethnic diversity as a good thing. Begin by asking questions. Learn from their experiences. A listening ear is usually welcomed and appreciated. In the process we learn about others, about people groups, about habits, about hopes and dreams, about cultures that are different from our own. It would be a blessing to see our churches filled by those from every tribe and language, people and nation (Revelation 5:9).

Persecution

Paul recorded these words in 2 Timothy 3:12: "Indeed, all who desire to live a godly life in Christ Jesus will be persecuted." According to Paul, persecution is inevitable for Christians. How that would be a motivating factor for sharing Christ seems farfetched. Imagine what Jesus' disciples thought when they heard these words afresh: "Blessed are you when others revile you and persecute you and utter all kinds of evil against you falsely on my account. Rejoice and be glad, for your reward is great in heaven, for so they persecuted the prophets who were before you" (Matthew 5:11-12).

Persecution is a sobering reality in the lives of Christians and sharing the gospel can lead to it. How is that for a rallying cry to get already fearful believers motivated to evangelize? Who among us desires to be imprisoned, beaten with rods, stoned, betrayed by our family and friends, ridiculed or martyred (2 Corinthians 11:23-33; Philippians 1:29-30)? Yet, ironically enough, the Church has experienced tremendous growth during times of extreme persecution and cruelty. In fact, God saw fit to establish the Church upon the greatest act of persecution, the tortuous death of his Son. Now, the Church continues to grow and be strengthened by the shed blood of martyrs.

The religious atmosphere in the United States and Canada is different from other parts of the world. Freedom of religion allows us to express our faith somewhat without fear of incarceration and punishment. Yet how long will this freedom last? The tide is turning, and Christians in North America may soon experience persecution for their faith as do many, many others around the world. Still, for the time being, our freedom is a great blessing, and an amazing opportunity.

Conclusion

There are many barriers and impediments to personal evangelism whether self-made or otherwise. The list is long, from stage fright, to insecurities about our biblical knowledge, ethnic and cultural diversity issues, fear of rejection, and just fear in general. All of these and many more can inhibit our evangelistic pursuits. As real as these issues are, they should not paralyze us and thereby ruin our witnessing opportunities. It is a privilege and a scared duty to share the good news of Jesus Christ. May we remain trusting and resting in our Savior, who gives us strength and hope for the task.

Discussion Questions

1. What is your greatest fear about your personal evangelism endeavors? Why?

2. How do you think you can either lessen your greatest fear or overcome it? Are you willing to establish accountability to help you with this? If so, when and how will you seek accountability?

3. Are you concerned about your reputation? How can sharing the law and the gospel potentially damage your reputation? Despite the potentially damaging effects to your reputation, are you still willing to share the law and the gospel?

4. What are some ethnic and cultural barriers that might concern you with regard to personal evangelism? What can you do to overcome those potential barriers?

5. What are some common objections to Christianity that you have heard? How would you answer those objections?

FOUR

DIGGING A BIT DEEPER: MUST I REALLY SHARE MY FAITH?

In 1932, composer Irving Berlin published the hit song, "Say It Isn't So." In it he sings,

"Everyone is saying you don't love me,
Say it isn't so.
Everywhere I go, everyone I know, whispers that you're
growing tired of me,
Say it isn't so.
People say that you found somebody new,
and it won't be long before you leave me,
Say it isn't true.
Say that everything is still okay,
that's all I want to know, and what they're saying,
Say it isn't so."

If this song were applied to the reasons people don't share their faith, it might go something like this:

"The demands are too great,
my concerns too overwhelming, and time is too precious,
Say it isn't so.
Leave it to the professionals, they know far more,
but if you're asking me to share my faith,
Say it isn't so.
Why me? I'm not fluid enough in my speech.
I know the Bible has something to say about my efforts,
Say it isn't true."

Corny as this song may sound, we can come up with a multitude of reasons to not share our faith. Personal evangelism does require a significant amount of time and energy. With all the commitments we presently maintain, it would be an added burden to share the gospel. There are many who share this opinion.

Many people have told me in conversation that their schedules are so jammed there is little time left to share the faith. For couples with young children, working 40-60 hour weeks, along with church responsibilities and school obligations, all factor in to the result of zero free time. If there were 10 hours extra every week, perhaps that would provide sufficient time for witnessing.

From university students to single parents and stay-at-home mothers, to physicians and seminarians, schedules seem jammed full. I can feel the same way at times. With a growing family to support, church responsibilities, publishing deadlines, and post-graduate work, my plate seems to overflow. But I have determined not to let any of these responsibilities overshadow the *privilege* to share Christ. Saying "I'm too busy" might also be masking my deeper worries and fears. "Say it isn't so."

Leave It Up to the Professionals

Doctors undergo extensive training for their profession, as do lawyers and other professionals. The same is true for pastors. There is rigorous study in systematic and biblical theology, Greek and Hebrew, counseling, apologetics, church history and a host of other vital subjects. The men leave seminary trained to teach and preach, and church members rely on them to get the job done, which often includes the work of evangelism.

Yet pastors may also struggle with sharing the faith. While they may be gifted preachers who feed the flock from Sunday to Sunday, many seldom get out much beyond the four walls of the church. Consequently their personal evangelism efforts are minimal. Time is a factor. Along with two sermons to prepare, they deal with counseling, home visitations, family commitments, teaching, prayer and study. But like the physician, stay-at-home mother, or seminary student, a busy schedule can also be code for deeper fears and anxieties. Although the call to the pulpit is strong, a minister may also feel uncomfortable talking to strangers about Christ. For the introverted, talking to anyone, let alone witnessing, does not come naturally. In the pulpit, services are regulated and controlled. In the public arena, there is a need to be spontaneous; to be ready for the unexpected. Rabbit trails are inevitable, tempers flare, and questions of effectiveness and giftedness surface. So, in everyday life, who should share their faith? This came up briefly in chapter 2, but let's dig deeper.

It Is Everyone's Privilege

How is sharing your faith a privilege? There are so many variables involved. On top of that, you probably have concerns about your giftedness, theological training (or lack thereof), comfort level, and many other issues. You are likely busy in the home, some of you may work full-time outside of the home, children keep your schedule full, and family vacations are often inserted into your schedule. All of these things matter and have a place in our daily living. Yet as Christians, sharing the gospel shouldn't be an afterthought, something we only do if we have time. It is our privilege to share the gospel and therefore time shouldn't work against us. Have you started humming the tune, "Say It Isn't So," yet?

Notice that I call it a privilege, not a "responsibility," as was done in previous chapters. In our day and age, responsibility is a term with negative connotations. For some it seems to negate the idea of "privilege." "Responsibility" can convey "duty" as opposed to "opportunity" and "privilege."

Look at it this way: the God of Creation has provided you with the truth, hidden from the eyes and hearts of so many. Yet he wants you to share that truth of redemption and of life in Christ with others who either fall in your path, or whom you seek out. Once captive and captivated by sin, you are now set free to help free others. Released from bondage to sin and newly captivated—made captive—to freedom in Jesus Christ, how can we not see this as a privilege to share in this work of life-saving for the glory of God, through the work of the Holy Spirit and for the sake of Jesus Christ, whose death and resurrection makes redemption possible and victory assured?

Since before the foundation of the world, God purposed to shower you with his love in Jesus Christ. "For God so loved the world," we are told, "that he sent his only begotten Son, that whosoever should believe in him shall not perish but have everlasting life" (John 3:16). That life has already begun for you! The beauty is that it is not only for you but for the whole world (1 John 2:1-2). We have the opportunity and privilege to share this message—the good news.

Paul's Exhortations

The apostle Paul recognized this privilege. Near the conclusion of his epistle to the Church at Colossae, he exhorts: "Walk in wisdom toward outsiders, making the best use of the time. Let your speech always be gracious, seasoned with salt, so that you may know how you ought to answer each person" (Colossians 4:5-6). Everyone within the body of Christ is called to "walk in wisdom toward outsiders." Paul's use of the word, "walk," is one that addresses the way Christians live and behave. Since walking is something we do regularly, so, too, our behavior toward non-Christians. Acting tactfully and behaving in a manner that is in keeping with our profession of faith and the name of Christ is something we need to do constantly in order to maintain our witness.

After Paul tells God's people to "walk in wisdom," he exhorts the Church to do it in such a way that "mak(es) the best use of the time" (Colossians 4:5b). In other words, our calling is to "redeem" or "appropriate" our time with unbelievers. How? By talking about Christ! This is not a suggestion but a command. Noted Greek scholar, Murray Harris, commenting on Colossians 4:5, writes: "[Christians] are to seize eagerly and use wisely every opportunity afforded them by time to promote the kingdom of God."[5] F. F. Bruce writes, "...each Christian has a special opportunity for witness and should make the most of it..."[6] P. T. O'Brien translates this verse, "Be

---

[5] Murray J. Harris, *Colossians and Philemon: Exegetical Guide to the Greek New* Testament (Grand Rapids: William B. Eerdmans Publishing Co., 1991), 197.

[6] F. F. Bruce, *The Epistles to the Colossians, to Philemon, and to the Ephesians* (Grand Rapids: William B. Eerdmans Publishing Company, 1984), 174.

wise in your behavior toward outsiders *by snapping up* every opportunity that comes" [italics mine].[7]

As opportunities arise, our speech should be gracious and seasoned with salt (4:6). Do not give an unbeliever reason to denounce Christ based on what you say or the way you live. We are to immerse ourselves in the grace that God exhibited to us in Jesus Christ. Only then will we be able to graciously answer the questions of unbelievers. Writes Murray Harris: In verse 6, "the emphasis [is on] perceptive answers that have that delicate blend of pungency and graciousness suited to the varying needs of individuals."[8]

While this book is not my public confession, I admit that I am very much a work in progress. My speech is not always laced with pungency and grace. There was a time when I purposefully scouted atheists and evolutionists with a view to arguing them into submission. My motto was, "I want to give you enough rope to hang yourself." That is not the best motto nor approach, I know. As a result, I frequently had hours of involved conversations that amounted to nothing more than shouting matches.

---

[7] P. T. O'Brien, *Colossians and Philemon* (Waco: Word, 1982), 235, 241. In his expanded paraphrase, Harris translates Colossians 4:5, "Be tactful and wise in all your relations with unbelievers; buy up every possible opportunity to influence them for the kingdom of God." Harris, *Colossians*, 198.

[8] Harris, *Colossians*, 198.

I've learned. Instead of thinking I want to argue you into submission, my approach is to ask questions. My reasoning is that if I am willing to listen to them, they will be more willing to listen to me. Nor do I look any longer for a certain type of person. Instead I am willing to engage with anyone around me. In doing so, I try to tailor-fit my words "to the varying needs of individuals."

Colossians 4:5-6 is not the only place Christians are exhorted to witness. Writing to the Church at Corinth, Paul said, "So, whether you eat or drink, or whatever you do, do all to the glory of God. Give no offense to Jews or to Greeks or to the church of God, just as I try to please everyone in everything I do, not seeking my own advantage, but that of many, that they may be saved. Be imitators of me, as I am of Christ" (1 Corinthians 10:31-11:1). That last exhortation of Paul's is critical for our understanding of personal evangelism.

This is where we can get into trouble, however. Perhaps you have heard the call to *be like Paul*. He seems to shatter the paradigm of Christian normalcy. From his unique conversion to the persecution he suffered, both from Jews and Greeks, Paul is the poster boy for radical Christianity. If there was ever an example of being "sold out" for Jesus, he was that man. The danger of a call to *be like Paul* is that we can lose ourselves in the process.

God equips us with certain gifts, to be used for his glory. When he wants us to imitate Paul, or anyone else, he will tell us. 1 Corinthians 10:31-11:1 is one of those places. Paul was active in pursuing others that they might come to saving faith in the Lord Jesus Christ. I repeat: Paul was active. So should we.

Too many people prefer the passive method—rest idly until someone approaches them about their faith (1 Peter 3:15). In my years of sharing the gospel with unbelievers, I can recount one instance when someone approached me about the Lord, but even this situation was created because of a previous conversation. This does not mean that it does not happen, but it is rare.

While a senior in college I was taking a communication studies class. The professor was engaging and cared about the students. At one point in the curriculum, we discussed the marketing techniques of Adolf Hitler. It was a lively, cordial conversation. During one class, a student asked, "Are Mormons Christian?" The professor said, "Yes." Immediately I raised my hand to differ. The ensuing debate lasted about five minutes.

Later in the semester, about the time of final exams, I gathered with a group of students to study. The library allowed space for open talks. Boy, did we talk. I don't know if we talked more about the final exam or something else. Either way, during that time, a young lady asked, "Can you tell me about Christianity?" This definitely had nothing to do with our final exam, but I found out later that the question was sparked by my previous debate with the professor over Mormonism. So was my experience entirely passive?

Paul actively pursued opportunities to share his faith with others. So must we. Sitting back and hoping people will ask us about our faith or come to our church may mean waiting a long time. While prayer is critical to personal evangelism efforts, it is also important that we open our mouths. P. T. O'Brien writes, "...the Corinthians, as Christian men and women, were to be committed to the gospel just as Paul was. They too should do everything for its sake, for like their apostle they were fellow-participants in its dynamic progress. They were to seek 'the advantage of the many,' that is, their salvation (10:33)."[9]

Paul's exhortation to the churches at Corinth and Colossae are clear. We must imitate Paul as we seek to bring others to Christ, buying up every opportunity to tell unbelievers about Christ and his kingdom. That may be terrifying, but necessary. Our comfort is not a prerequisite for anything that we do in the Christian life. The prerequisite, or the foundation, is Christ and his atoning work, and our obedience should follow.

Obedience, however, does not always imply a proper motive. Paul said, "Some indeed preach Christ from envy and rivalry, but others from good will... The former proclaim Christ out of selfish ambition, not sincerely but thinking to afflict me in my imprisonment" (Philippians 1:15, 17). Despite this insight into the human condition, Paul still rejoiced that Christ was preached (Philippians 1:18). He was not shocked by this

---

[9] P. T. O'Brien, *Gospel and Mission in the Writings of Paul: An Exegetical and Theological* Analysis (Grand Rapids: Baker Books, 1995), 106.

occurrence. In fact, more people were emboldened by Paul's imprisonment (Philippians 1:14). Paul approved of this activity, even though motives were not necessarily God-honoring.

The Church at Philippi was a partner in the gospel with Paul (Philippians 1:5). And this partnership was not limited to financial support, prayer, and encouragement (Philippians 1:19; 4:15-18). As did Paul, they actively suffered for the sake of the gospel (Philippians 1:27-30). They were exhorted to strive side by side for its sake (Philippians 1:27). This does not mean that their method of witnessing was identical to Paul's. Nevertheless, they were active in engaging an unbelieving world with Christ's message of hope.

What Now?

At this point you may have questions racing through your mind. It's not always easy to heed God's word and put it into practice. Our sins and fears can lead to avoidance. Do not lose heart. If you are willing to employ the gifts God has given you, you can begin to share the gospel and even invite others to church. You need not mirror the apostle Paul or Billy Graham in every way. This is about encouraging and equipping you to be who you are, with some stretching involved, by sharing the greatest news the world has ever known.

Discussion Questions

1. Have you been tempted to "leave it up to the professionals" to share the gospel? If so, why did that bring you comfort? If you have not been so inclined, why not?

2. How is sharing the gospel a privilege? Do you see it this way? Why, or why not?

3. According to the Bible passages quoted in this chapter, what are some scripture references that express the command for you to share the gospel? Will you obey?

4. Reflect back to chapter 1. Where should you start before even getting to the privilege of sharing the good news?

FIVE

PRAYER: AN IMPORTANT FACTOR IN THE EQUATION

Now that a brief overview of what the Bible says about sharing the faith has been presented, readers may be anxious to turn to some practical considerations. There are likely questions about what to say, about how to represent Christ accurately, and a laundry list of other items. As we go on from here we will get to those matters. First, however, a crucial element in the grand scheme of personal evangelism needs to be considered— the matter of prayer.

Two of the most difficult habits for a Christian to develop and work at, in my opinion, are personal evangelism and prayer. Christians are called to do both, but ultimately the results are beyond us. We rely on God to add his blessing according to his purposes. When we share our faith, God must still apply his grace to the hearts of unbelievers (John 3:3). Similarly when praying, we do so in expectation, but we also must wait on God to answer our prayers.

Prayer requests abound. People pray to overcome addictions, for humility, for financial stability, for perseverance in the faith, for safe travels, and for strong family life. These are just a few of the many, many prayer requests that go to the Father in the name of Jesus Christ every day. Prayer requests could easily fill volumes. Conscientious believers will pray for unsaved neighbors, for wandering family members, for church members and others in our circles of contact. But in the midst of such prayers, how often do we pray that God would grant us boldness to share the gospel with those unsaved neighbors, family members, and friends?

Prayer for Opportunities and Boldness

One of the joys of the Christian life should be our prayer life. The apostle Paul exhorts us to, "Let [our] requests be made known to God" (Philippians 4:6). The psalmist says, "The Lord is near to all who call on him, to all who call on him in truth" (Psalm 145:18). Indeed, those who are united to Christ by faith can stand confident that the Lord hears and answers prayers (1 John 5:14-15). He is not a spectator-God watching his creatures and his creation from afar. Rather, he loves us and is intimately concerned with our needs. God displays that great concern and love by having come to us in Jesus Christ and addressing our greatest need—a reconciled relationship with him. Through his Son he is pleased to grant us our petitions. What joy for us to know that the God of heaven and earth is willing to hear and answer prayers. As the old 1845 hymn by William Walford goes, "Sweet hour of prayer, sweet hour of prayer, the joys I feel, the bliss I share, of those whose anxious spirits burn with strong desires for thy return, with such I hasten to the place where God my savior shows his face, and gladly take my station there, and wait for thee, sweet hour of prayer."

Our interest in this chapter is not with knowing the joy of prayer, but with considering the content of prayer. It is easy for us to get into the custom (and rut) of praying for certain daily needs. An important question is, however, do we consider and pray for the needs of others, particularly unbelievers? While they may share the same material needs as anyone else, their greatest need is for salvation. What better way to turn our thinking toward personal evangelism than by praying for their salvation, for opportunities to share the gospel with them and to pray for boldness for ourselves to speak the words they need to hear.

For those who shy away from personal evangelism, the idea of praying to God in this way may be frightening, since we know that God answers in the affirmative when we pray according to his will (1 John 5:14-15). After reading chapter 4 we should be convinced that personal evangelism is his will. So the time is ripe for us to ask in faith and with conviction.

The apostle Paul has many things to teach us, but obviously, as stated earlier, we need not follow every means and method he utilized to spread the gospel. Yet there are of course certain things that we can and should duplicate. One example of his to draw on is his prayer life.

Paul was a missionary of missionaries. He traveled across the known world to make the gospel known. From the market place to the synagogues he preached Jesus Christ and him crucified (Acts 13:13-52; 1 Corinthians 2:2). For this apostle, to live was Christ and to die was gain (Philippians 1:21). All of his life's energies, post-conversion, were directed to make Christ known. Yet even this daring and adventurous apostle prayed for opportunities and boldness.

Paul says in Colossians 4:2-3, "Continue steadfastly in prayer, being watchful in it with thanksgiving. At the same time, pray also for us, that God may open to us a door for the word, to declare the mystery of Christ..." In Ephesians 6:18-20, the apostle says, "...keep alert with all perseverance, making supplication for all the saints, and also for me, that words may be given to me in opening my mouth boldly to proclaim the mystery of the gospel, for which I am an ambassador in chains, that I may declare it boldly, as I ought to speak." Paul requested that the Church pray that he be given opportunities to share Christ and that he would have the boldness to declare the gospel as he ought.

If Paul prayed this way, surely we should as well. Like Paul, we should pray that the Lord would provide opportunities to share our faith (Philippians 4:6). We know that God orchestrates all things. If this becomes a consistent prayer from our lips and heart, God will honor this request and provide an abundance of opportunities to talk about him to others. Consider making this a part of your daily prayers.

Remember also to pray for boldness. Sharing the gospel can be uncomfortable. We are sharing something that people don't want to hear. Concern for our reputation can also put a damper on our evangelistic endeavors. So boldness is needed. We need to ask God to help us overcome our personal impediments to share the good news.

Prayer for Humility

After praying for opportunities to share my faith and for the boldness to execute this endeavor, God blessed and answered my prayer positively. The problem for me was my lack of humility. I stood *over* the person instead of *beside* him. I was antagonistic in my conversation, acting as if I was better than him. Why did that happen?

While my theological database would have definitely screamed "No," my theology did not match my actions (Colossians 4:5-6). I had forgotten the place from which I came. I was not born a Christian. I was dead in trespasses and sins (Ephesians 2:1). God's wrath was upon me and I had no hope in and of myself (Isaiah 64:6;

89

John 3:36). But God! He sent someone in my path who graciously and humbly invited me to church. I went and God rescued me from the penalty of my sin and brought me into a justified state before him.

Did I deserve it? No. Neither was I interested in God, nor in being dependent on him. Did I earn it? No. Yet grace broke through in the form of Jesus Christ. He granted me his righteousness and favor and took upon himself the wrath that I deserved. This is my story.

So why, then, would I share the gospel in an antagonistic and prideful manner if I did nothing to earn salvation? I lacked humility. I added to the offense of the cross by my prideful presentation. Thus, it is essential to pray for humility. With me, ask the Lord to help us present the gospel in such a way as to accurately reflect the truths of the word and the love of God. Pray the Lord will help us realize more and more the magnitude of his grace and that we will be mindful of that grace as we tell others about Jesus Christ. Ask God, in the words of John the Baptist, that he might increase and we might decrease (John 3:30).

Prayer for Listening Ears

While I regret having made mistakes over the years regarding personal evangelism, I am glad that you can learn from me. As my mother used to say, "I am a good example of how not to be." You do not want to make the same mistakes I did.

Those who know me well know that I love to talk. In the vernacular it is called "running my mouth." Some people do not mind it but others may be less patient with me. Some people would rather listen than talk. There are others, like me, who prefer to talk. One thing my wife taught me was how to listen. Every time I had an issue I wanted to discuss, my wife patiently and lovingly sat back and listened. Her responses were sparing, but meaningful. She knows when to speak and when to listen.

My idea of listening, when my wife had something to share with me, was completing her sentences and providing a quick solution. This likely lessened her desire to talk even more. What I came to realize was that by not taking the time to listen fully, I did not hear her concerns completely. Although a woman of few words, I have learned a tremendous amount by observing her.

Prior to entering pastoral ministry, I was on a one-way track to medical school, something I wanted to do from my youth. My motive was to help others. But one day, a dear friend pulled me aside and warned me. Amid our conversation, he told me about the type of doctor he did not want me to be. He advised me to listen to my patients. "Do not be the type of physician who hears a few symptoms and immediately diagnoses the problem," he said. "Listen to your patient even if you have heard the symptoms a million times. Your patient's ailment might turn out to be something you did not expect," he declared.

This was great advice, which could be applied in many areas outside of patient diagnosis, but I did not apply that advice. This was reflected in the first several years of marriage. While a slow learner, I have begun to apply these principles in my personal life as well as in my personal evangelism. Though I have heard repeatedly the same concerns from unbelievers, I have learned to let them speak and to listen intently (Colossians 4:5). There may be nuances in their story different from others that may help me to more effectively minister to them. I cannot do this in my own strength! I still like to talk. I need the help of the Holy Spirit to help me to listen. Will you pray, as I do, for listening ears?

Prayer for Wisdom

When you pray for opportunities to share the gospel, the boldness to do it, a humble heart, and listening ears, you should also pray for wisdom. The apostle Paul writes, "Walk in wisdom toward outsiders, making the best use of the time" (Colossians 4:5). There is a connection between wisdom—the appropriate application of knowledge—and making the best use of time with outsiders (i.e., unbelievers).

Once while standing in line at a local ice cream shop in California, a young lady began engaging the cashier in a conversation about Christ. It started fairly simply and innocently. The cashier was respectful and did not seem to mind. The problem began as the line for ice cream lengthened. As several minutes passed and the line continued to grow, it became clear that this was not the best time to practice personal evangelism. The cashier had a job to do. Sometimes wisdom says, "Not now." As eager as we may be to share the gospel, we may have to wait and continue the conversation another time. There may also be times when you cannot invite someone to church or share the gospel immediately. For some reason, the person is adverse to matters of religion (Matthew 7:6). Therefore, depending on the situation, wisdom may dictate that you need to establish a deeper relationship first. Once established, an invitation to church and sharing the gospel may be the next step.

Wisdom also provides insight into how to share the gospel. The message itself does not change, but the approach taken is flexible. For example, after listening to a person share about her life's situation, you may discover that her father was absent. Do you want to lightly gloss over the love of God in light of her situation, or perhaps stress the Father's abundant love in Jesus Christ? (John 3:16; Romans 5:8). In your petitions, remember to pray that God would grant you wisdom in your evangelistic activities.

Prayer for Open Hearts

During one of Paul's missionary journeys, Luke records, "And on the Sabbath day we went outside the gate to the riverside, where we supposed there was a place of prayer, and we sat down and spoke to the women who had come together. One who heard us was a woman named Lydia, from the city of Thyatira, a seller of purple goods, who was a worshiper of God. The Lord opened her heart to pay attention to what was said by Paul" (Acts 16:13-14). Unless God moves the hearts of men and women, the message of Christ will serve to harden hearts (John 12:37-40; Romans 1:28; 9:18). Pray that God would be merciful to those with whom we share the gospel. We must pray that, by his Holy Spirit, he will enlighten the hearts of the blind to receive the message of hope, just as he did to Lydia.

Recall your own conversion if you are able. Perhaps you have walked with the Lord most of your life and cannot remember a day when you did not know Christ as Savior. There may be others who can recall a moment when the Lord allowed you to receive him as he is presented in the gospel. Either way, there was a time when your heart was hardened, and God, by his grace, opened your blind eyes and exposed you to his love in Jesus Christ. What a blessing! What a privilege!

For years, I prayed for my mother. Virtually with every conversation, I tried to talk about the Lord. At some points, she was hostile to Christ and his word. The law exposed her utter sinfulness and she rebelled against realizing who she was before God. Things became discouraging. "If the Lord will save anyone," I pleaded, "please save my mother." As time went on, things did not look hopeful from my perspective.

Then one day she told me about reading a short booklet on justification. She said that she agreed with its contents. I was stunned. Several conversations later, she told me that she had been reading *Table Talk* magazine and needed to look up the term, "adiaphora." I was shocked by the change.

God displayed his mercy in her life. Like Lydia, he opened her heart to hear and receive the good news of Christ. Not too much later I preached at the church service where she made her public profession of faith. Praise God! I am thankful that I will one day see my mother in heaven. God is able and mighty to save. While we may not see results immediately, and perhaps not even in our lifetime, continue to pray that the Lord would open the hearts of those with whom we share the good news. He is faithful!

Conclusion

The importance of prayer in our evangelistic activities can easily be overlooked. It takes time and effort, but it is vital and well worth it. The God of heaven and earth gives us the privilege of prayer—access to the Father, through the Son, with the Holy Spirit's intercession. Not only does he allow us to pray, he also listens to our prayers. What a blessing! What a privilege! What an opportunity! Let's remember to pray for opportunities to share our faith, for boldness to do it, for a humble attitude, for listening ears, for wisdom, and for open hearts to receive the good news.

Discussion Questions

1. Why is prayer important in personal evangelism? Is it sometimes overlooked? If so, why?

2. Do you see a need to pray for some of the items listed in this chapter? Which ones and why?

3. Why is humility necessary in personal evangelism?

4. As you pray for opportunities to share your faith, what are some opportunities that might presently be available?

Six

THE CHURCH: A GOOD SEGUE

What is one of your favorite things to do? Having been raised in Las Vegas, if asked during my teenage years, my answer was simple. No, not gambling, but eating in casino restaurants. For little money, I could eat until my belly ached. This was quite a deal, especially because we did not have much money. When raised on welfare one barely has enough food to eat, so a $5 buffet becomes a feast.

What about you? Is it having a meal with your spouse or best friend? Do you enjoy traveling or playing sports? Reading? Sleeping? Hiking? Personal quiet time, perhaps? Everyone enjoys doing something, and normally what people enjoy doing most, they love to talk about.

Although I no longer live in Las Vegas, I still enjoy eating. I love trying new food, as long as it is not spicy, and I particularly enjoy eating new food with my wife. But something changed between my teenager years and now. I became a Christian. God blessed me with his greatest gift—the Lord Jesus Christ. Now while I still like to eat, that is not one of my favorite things to do. As a Christian, I love going to church. There is nothing like it! Each Sunday I have the privilege to spiritually feed upon Christ in the preaching of the word and the administration of the sacraments. In church, the promises of God are proclaimed. The good news is that he is for me and not against me. Yet these promises are not merely for me as an individual, but for his Church. The congregation is called into God's presence, and by his grace, we have communion with him and with each other (Hebrews 12:18-29). This is what I love and enjoy doing, and what people enjoy they are happy to talk about. For me, church is a source of easy conversation.

What do others enjoy discussing? Stand in line at the grocery store or post office and you'll quickly find out. Not too long ago, every conversation seemed to be about the federal election. "Whom are you supporting?" "Why are you voting for him?" "Is it worth bothering to vote at all?" Living in the southeast, in the heart of Civil War territory, many conversations took place daily. They were often passionate conversations from people with strong convictions.

With the same kind of passion, Christians should be able to talk about the Church, but not in a critical way. There is enough of that going around. Rather, conversations about worship should be positive and edifying. What did you learn from the sermon? Why are you thankful for the gospel? Why do you enjoy the prayers and singing? How does the fellowship bless you? Don't merely say these things to fellow Christians, but share your thoughts with unbelievers as well.

A Good Segue

Since religion is one of the subjects we are told to avoid discussing, getting into a conversation about church and the gospel can be difficult. "Keep your religion to yourself," people say. Of course this is contrary to scripture. While religion may be personal, it is not private. The question is not, "Should I talk about church and my faith," but, "How do I get it into a conversation about them?"

Some people settle for the corny route, asking, "Would you like a drink of water? Have you heard of the Living Water?" Others take the direct approach by saying to a neighbor, "Let me tell you about Jesus." Some hand out gospel tracts, while others stand on a soapbox on a street corner, knock on doors, or build relationships with people and then share the gospel with them. Still others might set up a booth at a community fair or other public venue. Perhaps you have tried some of these methods. Perhaps you are still waiting to take the plunge.

Wherever you find yourself, there is a safe and comfortable way to get a conversation started about Christ and his Church. Even the most timid, introverted person can attempt this.

Before unfolding this idea, some words of caution are in order. This "formula" can easily become sterile if applied in a mechanical manner. If that becomes the case, then you are no longer viewing the person being approached as a human being, but more as the target of a method. You are simply there "to do a job" and move on. This is definitely not the way to go.

For years I enjoyed sharing my faith and talking about Christ's Church using a certain paradigm. No matter what people said regarding their objections or concerns about the state of the Church, it was as if I did not hear them. My job was to make it through the formula. There was a list of questions to ask, a number of statements to make, and a concluding comment, "Repent and believe the good news." Not all people who use a particular paradigm fall into this trap, but I did. I realize now that I was more concerned with saying the right things instead of listening to the people. And while I did care about the people, there was a certain level of caring that was absent in my approach because I was not genuinely listening to those with whom I shared Christ. I elevated the evangelistic paradigm above their sincere concerns. So, once again, don't do what I did. Take the time to listen to responses offered and answer them accordingly (Colossians 4:5-6).

Now let's turn to the method of turning a conversation around to the subject of Christ and his Church. It's simple, and it starts with the question, "How are you?" We all say this pat phrase when we meet someone. To some degree, it's woven into the fabric of our society. It's a matter of common courtesy. It's a way of showing an interest in people's well-being. "How are you?" we ask, as we walk by our neighbors. "How are you?" we inquire as we pay for an oil change. "How are you?" we say, as we sit next to someone on an airplane. It's a basic and commonplace question that follows easily after "hello."

On one of those rare trips to the grocery store, I stood in line waiting to pay. On this occasion, I asked the woman at the checkout counter, "How are you?" Her response was unforgettable. She responded with tears, tears that came before her words.

With eyes moist, she looked at me and said, "No one has asked me that in months." I did not know what to say. Her comment caught me off-guard. Normally I have a response for a good many things, but not this time. Why had no one asked her how she was doing? Perhaps it's not as commonplace as I'd like to believe. Have we become that cold? Are these types of things no longer being taught in the home?

I don't have the answer to those questions, but one thing is certain: she was keeping track. She watched hundreds of people walk by her without any of them extending the simple courtesy of inquiring into her day. Thankfully, she stopped crying and we had a brief conversation. I do not remember all of the details, but I know it was fruitful because the topic transitioned to Christ and his Church. It all started by asking a simple question, "How are you?"

How So?

When someone asks, "How are you?" the usual response is, "I'm well," simply to move the conversation forward. On occasion some may be more transparent and lay their lives out there. They might tell someone they are feeling lousy or are having problems with their children. Whatever the response, a conversation is initiated. And normally, after you ask someone, "How are you?" they respond in kind.

There are several response options. You can say, "Fine," and the conversation ends there. You can respond by relating something that happened to you recently (e.g., your children returned to school, your child just started walking, etc.). Or you can talk about another highlight of the week: the Church! Remember that people talk about what they enjoy, and if the Church is something you thoroughly enjoy, you can talk about it—you have a conversation starter.

My wife and I have a saying: "We live from Sunday to Sunday." As much as we love spending time together, the highlight of our week is Sunday. This is the only time that we get a glimpse of heaven. The Lord Jesus speaks to us through the reading and preaching of his word, as well as through the sacraments. We are reminded of the grace of God in Jesus Christ and our union with him. No matter what happens in this life, "nothing can separate us from the love of God in Christ" (Romans 8:39). He promised that he would never leave us nor forsake us (Hebrews 13:5-6). He is a good God; he is our God, the only true and living God. What could be better?

You may be thinking, "I enjoy church, too. In fact, I believe everything you have said about church. But how do I take the conversation from, "How are you?" to talking about Christ and his Church?" Here is how.

After someone asks you, "How are you?" answer honestly. But get out of the habit of merely saying, "Fine." Open up as much as you're willing. People appreciate transparency. If things are or are not going well, share what's on your heart. Quite possibly the person to whom you are speaking is going through something similar. This might be a time to encourage each other. It's in the midst of your response that you can bring up church. If it is Monday, for example, you can say, "I am well. Thanks for asking. I had an especially good weekend because of what happened in church yesterday." Or if it is Friday, you can say, "I'm great! I'm looking forward to the weekend because of church." Those who are interested will naturally follow up with a questioning response. Those who wish to avoid church talk will move on to something else. But you've given them an opportunity to probe.

After injecting church attendance into the conversation, the person's facial expression will tell you something about his thoughts on the subject of religion. Perhaps the person will respond, "I went to church, too." Or the person may appear distant and quiet. There are a number of possible responses, both verbal and non-verbal, but much can be told by their initial reaction.

If silence follows, you might try another question. You could ask, "Do you go to church?" Or as a buffer or bridge, your response could be, "I hope I did not offend you by bringing up church. I know some people do not like to talk about that subject." If the person responds, "Yes, that was fine," you can follow up with, "Do you attend church?" The conversation becomes more focused.

If the person does go to church, the next question would be to find out where he goes. Additional questions would help to find out the level of commitment: "How long have you attended?" and "What do you like best about your church? These questions reveal a genuine curiosity on your part and will tell you a lot about the person to whom you are speaking.

If the answer is, "I don't go to church," an opportunity opens up, either for an invitation to your church or a further exploration of the person's beliefs and value system. If an invitation to church is offered, be prepared to follow up. I carry business-sized "Join Us" cards with our church logo, service times, address, and a map on the back. They are convenient and easily accessible. Also, when I do extend an invitation to church, it generally includes an invitation for lunch afterward at our home. This provides an opportunity to get to know the person better. One might also consider offering a ride to church just to be sure that you will see him that Sunday.

This is a non-threatening way to engage people in order to converse about spiritual matters. I use this, or a variation of it, quite often when I'm in the marketplace. With my next-door neighbors, or those in my immediate housing community, I sometimes approach things a bit differently.

Often our neighbors know we're Christians. Whether it's our t-shirts, bumper stickers, or our early departure every Sunday morning, there are certain clues that we're churchgoers. If I have not yet spoken to my neighbors about Christ and his Church, I attempt to cross that frontier in several ways.

Sometimes I'm direct. I will approach my neighbor, cordially greet him, and ask if he will attend church with me. The conversation might go something like this. "Sam, I know we've never crossed this barrier; what do you think about church? I attend and I'd love for you to accompany my family one Sunday morning." I use this appeal if I think, based on previous interactions, my neighbor won't overreact. However, I can't, with absolute certainty, predict every response.

Another way to approach your neighbor about church is to engage her over the latest religious controversy or event. Unfortunately, there's always a religious scandal or event in the news. It makes people curious as to the authenticity of Christianity. How could we who say we believe in a risen Savior act in a pagan manner? When you see your neighbor, greet her. Ask her how she's doing. Engage in normal small talk. Then interject the latest religious controversy. The election of the pope was a great conversation piece. Many people had some idea that was taking place, and all we, as Christians, needed to do was ask our neighbor, "What do you think about the pope's election?" Allow the conversation to develop from there.

National holidays are another tool you can use to talk to your neighbors about church and invite them. The obvious holidays are Easter and Christmas. Halloween is a great national holiday, too. In fact, it's a bit more convenient because your neighbors come to you.

On this particular October 31st, as children and parents arrived at our home, my wife and I gave them candy and gospel tracts. As parents noticed us putting tracts into their children's candy bags, they often asked, "What's that?" This gave us a perfect opportunity to share the gospel. This was not always the case, however. Many tracts were placed into bags, which did not provide the opportunity to share Christ. Our hope, in that case, is that when parents inspect their children's candy, they will find the tract, and the seed of the gospel will be firmly planted.

Sometimes we see the fruit of our labors and other times we won't. By God's grace, this time we did. The next day, my wife and I received a knock at our door. When I opened the door, a lady stood there and asked me if I was the one who gave out the gospel tracts. I answered, "Yes." Once this was affirmed, she proceeded to tell me why my method of telling others about Jesus using tracts was rude and uncompassionate because the tract mentioned hell. She said, "Every time I hear about Jesus, he is compassionate, loving, and never talks about hell." I began to tell her about my Lord and how, at times, he did mention things that were hard to hear.

As the conversation continued, I asked her, "Are you a Christian?" She replied, "No, I'm Jewish." After this brief exchange, I invited her into our home. Our conversation progressed to small talk (e.g., where are you from? How long have you lived here?). As she told my wife and I these things, I invited her over for dinner. She accepted.

As our interaction came to a close, I asked her, "What exactly did you think you were going to accomplish today?" She responded, "I thought I was going to tell you how you were wrong and why you need to change your approach." To this, I responded, "And now?" "I realized I was wrong," she said. Immediately after this, she said some extremely surprising things. "Can I be honest with you?" she asked. "I read the back of that card you gave me and for a moment I thought, 'I wonder if this is right.'" I couldn't believe she said this, but she continued. "And since I'm being honest, I may as well tell you this. I frequently wonder if Jesus is who he said he is."

During our conversation, I invited her into our home for a meal. Hospitality is a great a tool you can utilize to help interact with your neighbors about Christ's Church. This, too, is a non-threatening way to get a sense of where they stand regarding religious matters. And even if you don't bring up the Church during your

107

neighbor's first visit to your home, they will likely get a sense that you are religious by the paintings on your wall or the Bible on your table. The first visit may simply lay the groundwork for future conversations, but Lord willing, you will have the opportunity to bridge that gap. (I get into more detail about hospitality in chapter 8).

Variation to the "Paradigm"

The danger of any planned approach is that it becomes formulaic, like a three-step guide to achieving your potential. You may fall into a rote pattern that appears robotic and unnatural. If you are going to use any of the aforementioned approaches, make it your own. In other words, be you! God has gifted each of us in unique ways. So don't do as I do, but do as you do. Use the ideas mentioned and make them your own. Initiate a conversation in a way that makes you comfortable and is natural to your personality. Whatever you do, keep in mind that you are only one small step from entering into a conversation about spiritual matters. All it takes is one question or comment and the door may swing open to an evangelistic possibility.

I sat in a Starbucks one afternoon to work on my sermon and post-graduate assignments. My table was filled with books. A gentleman waiting for his coffee struck up a conversation on education with the Starbuck's employee. During the conversation he said to the employee, as he looked at all my books, "I remember when I used to fill my head with useless information." Was he talking about me? It seemed like he was, but I chose to ignore it, until he sat directly behind me.

Instead of starting the conversation by saying, "How are you?" I took a more forthright approach. I leaned back to him and said, "The information I am studying is not useless." That was my icebreaker. The way I began the conversation lent itself to my personality. I can be upfront when I think necessary. Thankfully, he did not take offense. He responded with, "I was not talking about you. Your books reminded me of what I learned in engineering school." He went on to say that much of the stuff he learned is now useless. Crunching numbers and memorizing paradigms means nothing to him.

The conversation then turned from his work as an engineer to his children. He shared information about his three children and the mistakes that he made raising them. He mentioned his current occupation, the fact that he is divorced and happy as a single man, and many other things. Eventually, in the midst of a 45-minute conversation, I brought up church. I told him my occupation—a pastor. (One advantage of being a pastor is that you can get into spiritual conversations easily). The rest of the time was spent talking about Christ and his Church. I shared the law and the gospel with him, invited him to church, and asked how I could pray for him.

The point is that you do not have to follow, word-for-word, the examples provided. There are many ways

109

to enter into a conversation. Simply keep in mind that the Church is a good segue to converse about spiritual matters. And remember, this can be with someone whom you've just met or someone with whom you already have a relationship. All it takes is a simple question, "How are you?" and see where it goes from there!

Discussion Questions

1. Is attending church one of your favorite things to do? Why? Why not?

2. How is the Church a good segue to start a conversation about spiritual matters? Take time to role-play potential conversations utilizing the principles provided in this chapter.

3. What are some variations to the, "How are you?" paradigm?

4. Are you willing to apply the principles used in this chapter on a daily or weekly basis? If so, will you ask someone to keep you accountable?

5. Can you recall a situation where you applied the principles taught in this chapter? Explain.

SEVEN

GLOOM AND GLORY: THE LAW AND THE GOSPEL

The last chapter was meant to get the ball rolling, to begin the transition from theory to practice, from the idea of personal evangelism to the doing of personal evangelism, if even in a small way. Asking the simple question, "How are you?" should roll easily off your tongue, but transitioning the conversation from small talk to the Church might be where you need to exert yourself. If you are not accustomed to talking about the Church in everyday conversation, this may take some effort. And the good thing is, this approach is not offensive to many. Hopefully that will put you at ease. But allow me to be the bearer of bad news. The Church is extremely important. In fact, every Christian should be a member of a Bible-believing church. The epistles were written to churches. In the book of Acts, people were baptized and added to the church. We were saved as individuals but added to a community. So inviting people to church is invaluable, but that is not personal evangelism. The most intimidating part still lies ahead.

Whether you are in line at the grocery store or speaking with your neighbor, at some point in the conversation you may have the privilege to take the conversation beyond an invitation to church, to the particulars of what is being taught *in* church—the law and the gospel.

Although this is the hardest part, please keep going. By way of encouragement, it is not as bad as you may think. Talking about the holiness of God, the unrighteousness of men, the depth of our sin, the debt we owe, eternal punishment, and the goodness of God in Christ as the only means of reconciliation with God are all tough subjects. Yet if approached correctly, there is less to fear than you may think, especially when you realize how much there is going for you.

You Have Many Things Going for You

I am assuming that everyone reading this book attends a church. Every Sunday the law and the gospel (or what I call, "Gloom and Glory") are preached. The law reminds us of our sin. In thought, word, and deed, we have transgressed God's law. There is no escaping the crushing weight of it. Before God we are guilty—gloom. Yet there is hope for release from the crushing weight of the law. It is the message of the gospel preached to God's people. "But God shows his love for us in that while we were sinners, Christ died for us" (Romans 5:8). "Greater

114

love has no one than this, that someone lay down his life for his friends" (John 15:13). "The saying is trustworthy and deserving of full acceptance, that Christ Jesus came into the word to save sinners..." (1 Timothy 1:15)—glory.

No message throughout the world and in all human history can remotely compare. In Christ, there is complete forgiveness of sins, your guilt transferred to Jesus; his righteousness given to you. Although at one time the law was your enemy, you can now delight in it (Psalm 1:2; 19:7-10; 40:8). By the grace of God, it directs you; rejoice in the direction it provides.

Not so for unbelievers. The God of all creation is not their friend but their enemy. His wrath abides upon them, and if they are not reconciled to God, their ultimate destination is the lake of fire (John 3:36; Revelation 20:11-15). All that stands between them and eternal destruction is the last enemy—death.

This is an unpopular message. Yet it must be shared. Thankfully you know this message. It may not come out of your mouth without your lips quivering, but the power is in the message—the gospel—and not how smoothly you convey it. What you have going for you is your familiarity with the message of everlasting life. Not only do you know it on account of your personal Bible reading, but also since you attend church regularly, the law and the gospel are reinforced every Sunday. Every Sunday is a training ground for sharing the law and the glorious gospel of Jesus Christ!

Your other ally is the image of God. Although we are no longer born in true righteousness and holiness (Ephesians 4:24), his stamp is still on us. Each of us bears a partial resemblance to the Lord. The problem is, without Christ, we suppress that resemblance. We want nothing to do with God. Yet despite such distain for our Creator, we cannot escape his mark. The apostle Paul says that the work of the law is written on our hearts (Romans 2:15). The reason we know right and wrong is because God put that knowledge within us. The ability to discern good from evil and right from wrong is not an evolutionary development or something that originates with our parent(s). Our parent(s) simply reinforce what God placed within us. So where can we go to escape that divine image within us?

The problem is that it's mixed with the image of Adam (Genesis 5:3). Our sinful tendency is to disregard the divine image within and side with the first man, Adam. The flesh (our old nature) fights against the spirit. When our flesh screams, we often want to obey it. "Silence the flesh by giving into its temptations," we think. "It's too much to bear. Obey the lusts of the flesh and things will quiet down," we say. This struggle is common to all of us. To various degrees, both believers and unbelievers know what is right and wrong. When confronted with the law, we must admit we've all broken it. Since this is commonplace, we have another ally: compassion.

We know what it's like to disobey God, and what it's like to fight against our true identity and follow after

116

the course of this world; to be constantly drawn away from the Lord to fulfill the lusts of the flesh. The war is real (Ephesians 6:10-20) and the fight is to stay along the path of the righteous. But how is this reality related to your ally, compassion?

Hebrews talks about the great high priesthood of Jesus. "For we do not have a high priest who is unable to sympathize with our weaknesses, but one who in every respect has been tempted as we are yet without sin" (Hebrews 4:15). Although Jesus obeyed perfectly every aspect of the law, he was still tempted as we are. He understands us. He recognizes the influence of sin and can sympathize with us.

Far better than a wife knows her husband or a father his child, Christ knows us, loves us, and gave himself up for us. He "did not count equality a thing to be grasped, but he emptied himself, by taking the form of a servant, being born in the likeness of men. And being found in human form, he humbled himself by becoming obedient to the point of death, even death on a cross" (Philippians 2:6-8). What manner of love and compassion is this? He became like us, of his own accord, so that we can become sons of God.

In 1 Corinthians 6:9-10, Paul lists a cluster of sins (e.g., sexual immorality, drunkenness, idolatry, etc.). After this list, he says, "And such were some of you" (v. 11). In Christ, you are no longer what you were because "you were washed, you were sanctified, you were justified in the name of the Lord Christ and by the Spirit of our God" (v. 11).

God in Christ had compassion on us. He became like us to experience the trials of this world, but also to overcome sin, Satan, and death. Can we have compassion on others in a similar way (1 Corinthians 9:19-23)? Can we relate to others since we know the struggle that sin brings—the temptations, the guilt, the shame? Yet while we recognize the need for a Savior, they do not. In that significant sense, we differ. The Spirit of the living God has regenerated us (John 3:3). We, as Christians, share something they need—the hope of Christ in the gospel!

So the task is clear. Knowing their bleak situation and their ultimate destination, what we need to remember is that because Christ had compassion on us, that Christ-like compassion should flow from us to others. Our compassion should be evident. In one of my witnessing encounters, Sam seemed to think so.

One day, after street preaching on a local college campus, I interacted with several students. It was an atypical crowd. Gays, lesbians, and supporters of homosexual marriage surrounded me. One lady from my church said it was comparable to "the lion's den." Still, I had a pleasant conversation with them. Later that day I received this email.

My name is Sam. We met earlier today at the university campus and I really enjoyed speaking with you about your religious beliefs. Just a little about myself: I was raised Muslim but no longer identify with Islam or with any specific religion. Though I find many teachings of the Koran truly beautiful and I acknowledge that, to some extent, the fundamental teachings of Islam have shaped my moral code and my mindset itself, I have never felt any sense of a significant connection with 'God.' I now ascribe to the religion of "Open-Mindedness." A year ago, I would've felt disdain towards you while hearing you publicly preach your Christian beliefs. Instead, as I told you earlier, I felt nothing but compassion and most of all curiosity. I like to believe that I am now on a spiritual journey and I would love to engage in more dialogue with you if possible.

The compassion that he felt went a long way, enough for him to carry on the conversation. Remember that it is our ally.

A final point going for us is our effectiveness. While some of us are new to personal evangelism, the reality is that we are 100% effective when we share God's word in evangelistic encounters. Despite our weaknesses, when the word of God is used to share the law and the gospel, *we are effective*. Recall the words of the prophet Isaiah. "For as the rain and the snow come down from heaven and do not return there but water the earth, making it bring forth and sprout, giving seed to the sower and bread to the eater, so shall my word be that goes out from my mouth; it shall not return to me empty, but it shall accomplish that which I purpose, and shall succeed in the things for which I sent it" (Isaiah 55:10-11).

The right use of God's word will accomplish all that he intends. From the moment we begin talking about the gospel with others, God will do what he has purposed, which, we hope, is to draw that individual or individuals to himself (John 6:44).

We know God's word is effective intellectually, yet over the years I have had to answer this same question many times: "How effective is this [your personal evangelism]?" In my own practice I have become more and more confident in God's word and its effectiveness when sharing the good news. I may not be effective in myself, for example, by not saying things very well, or by not answering every question as thoroughly as it deserves. Yet my confidence is in the effectiveness of God's word, and that is rock solid. So when we share the good news of Christ, we are always effective. Given all of this knowledge, we do have much going for us!

What Now?

Where do we go from here? How do we take a conversation from small talk to the law and the gospel? Since we previously outlined how to engage others in conversation about the Church, we can assume that part of the conversation has already occurred. The transition is now to the Church's central teaching—the law and the gospel.

This may not all take place in a line at the grocery store, although it can. It depends on how much time is available. The cashier's time is limited (but you can also talk to those in front of or behind you). Nevertheless, you want to be mindful of your surroundings and time restraints. If you strike up a conversation with the cashier, be considerate and realize that he is on the clock, and he is not being paid to converse at length about religious matters. Your invitation to church, and perhaps exchanging email addresses, might be the introduction to a more lengthy conversation later.

If, however, you do have time to talk about God's law and his Christ (e.g., with a neighbor, while on a lunch break, after work with a co-worker, etc.), you can transition the conversation from an invitation to church to the weightier truths of scripture.

The next question to ask is simply, "May I share with you what I believe about God?" The ball is now in his court. A "yes" answer opens the door. A "no" answer can lead to the question, "Did I offend you?" with the additional, "If I did, I did not mean to." This extends compassion and relates empathy. You know what it is like to be presented with something you may not necessarily want to hear. There are times when even Christians do not want to hear the truths of scripture. How much more the unbeliever? Therefore, if he says "no" to your question, the conversation is still open. Now he has the opportunity to express what is on his heart. Regardless of his response, you made an attempt to bring up the things of God!

If this conversation takes place at a grocery store, this person likely lives in your community. Regardless of how they responded to your invitation to church and the presentation of the gospel, always be friendly. Keep the lines of communication open. Always ask the person how he or she is doing. This individual now knows you are a Christian. This may open the door for future conversations.

If, however, you were attempting to engage your neighbor or unbelieving family member using these principles, the likelihood of this type of conversation unfolding again is higher. Everyone needs someone with whom they can speak when they have questions about religion. Most people want to talk with someone they trust, a sympathetic ear. Often people will seek you out for answers to their religious questions once they know you are a Christian. Just make sure they know this, not simply because they see you leaving early Sunday mornings, because you wear Christian shirts, or have bumper stickers on your car, but because you have attempted to engage them with an invitation to church and the law and the gospel.

Another path to narrow the conversation to matters of gloom and glory is to ask people what they know about the Bible. Particularly, you can ask them, "What do you think the central teaching of the Bible is?" This is especially helpful with those who have even the smallest understanding of Christianity. Perhaps they were raised in church but later rebelled. Maybe the individual went to church or Vacation Bible School once or twice. This question allows you to explore the depth of this individual's knowledge of the Bible with the end in view—Christ crucified.

More Particulars

Remember that many people are not exposed to Christianity. They don't read the Bible, attend worship, or understand the concept of sin. Words such as "justification," "gospel," "sanctification," are foreign to them. "God" and "Jesus Christ" are used primarily in a vulgar way. Those who have heard of Jesus may perhaps have concluded that he was a good teacher, or someone to emulate. All the things that we have been taught from the Bible they view as foreign.

Therefore, the terms we use as we speak to others about the gospel must be simple and understandable. Asking someone, "May I share the gospel with you?" is probably not the best approach. They likely don't know what "gospel" means. So keep it simple. Unless the person with whom you are talking tells you that they have an understanding of Christianity, use basic terms and explain what you understand by those terms.

This book began with God. Similarly, when in a witnessing conversation, God should be presented early in the conversation, but be sure to explain who God is, what he is like, and why it matters.

The paradigm I utilize in personal evangelism encounters is: God as Creator, God as Judge, and God as Redeemer. "In the beginning," Genesis says, "God created the heavens and the earth" (Genesis 1:1). From

123

just one verse, it is evident that God describes himself as the Creator. As we continue reading Genesis 1, God also describes himself as the sustainer of life (Genesis 1:3-31; cf. John 1:3; Colossians 1:15-17). The first chapter provides a snapshot of who God is and what he is like. After The Fall, God reveals himself as Judge. Adam is judged for his violation of God's law. Any violation of God's law is sin (1 John 3:4). God asked, "Have you eaten of the tree of which I commanded you not to eat?" (Genesis 3:11). In Genesis 2:17, God provided one prohibition (his law): "…of the tree of the knowledge of good and evil you shall not eat, for in the day that you eat of it you shall surely die." When Adam disobeyed, he deserved eternal condemnation. But God! He revealed himself as the Redeemer of the fallen (Genesis 3:15, 21). When there was no hope, God provided hope. When death for Adam and Eve was inevitable, God bought life with his own blood.

A similar paradigm is observed in Acts 17. When Paul witnessed to the people of Athens, he said, "For as I passed alone and observed the objects of your worship, I found also an altar with this inscription, "To the unknown god." What therefore you worship as unknown, this I proclaim to you. The God who made the world and everything in it, being Lord of heaven and earth, does not live in temples made be man…" (Acts 17:23-24). The men of Athens worshiped a god, but not the true and living God. Paul makes a distinction between their false god and the God of heaven and earth, the creator and sustainer of life (Acts 17:24-26). This distinction
124

revealed their sin. They were not acting in accordance with the purpose for which they were created (Matthew 22:36-39; Acts 17:24-27; Romans 2:15). They worshiped and served a false god. The result of their sin was judgment (Acts 17:30-31). But in view of God's mercies, there was good news! "[God] has given assurance to all by raising [Christ] from the dead" (Acts 17:31).

At the conclusion of Paul's evangelistic encounter, some mocked him, while others were willing to hear Paul again, and some also believed (Acts 17:32-34). As it was with Lydia one chapter earlier, God opened the eyes of the blind, turning hearts of stone into hearts of flesh, from unbelief to the true and living God, the creator and sustainer of heaven and earth.

One morning on an airplane trip home from North Carolina, I was one of the last to board. If you have ever had that experience, people tend to stare at the last one coming in, perhaps wondering why it took that person so long to board.

The seats were three to a side. My seat was in the middle, between two large, wide-bodied men. I had to squeeze between them in order to sit down. The interesting part followed the greetings. When I told them, "This is my seat," one of the men said, "We were hoping no one was going to sit here." That took me aback. My response was, "So you better have some good conversation, then."

As I was putting my luggage in the overhead compartment, I asked, "What do you want to talk about: politics or religion?" One man said, "I don't like talking

125

about religion. How about politics?" I responded, "Okay."

Forty-five minutes into the flight the men were going back and forth about politics. I listened. Finally, one man noticed and asked, "Are you going to get involved in this conversation?" I said, "I don't want to talk about politics." He responded, "What, then?" I eagerly replied, "I want to talk about religion." He said, "Fine."

For nearly the remainder of the flight, I took them from Genesis to Revelation unfolding the purposes of God for his people. I told them that God is holy, righteous, and just (Isaiah 6:1-6; Jeremiah 12:1; Psalm 7:11; 25:8). I shared that he is the one true and living God, and there is no God besides him (Isaiah 44:6). It is this God who created them (Genesis 1:26-27; John 1:3). He did so with a purpose, but that purpose is neglected (Matthew 22:37-39; 1 John 1:8). "You do not love God with all of your heart, soul, and mind. You do not love your neighbor as yourself. God demands perfection from you in how you worship him and how you treat your neighbors." "Secondly," I told them, "God sees your every motive and thought. He even demands perfection in the inward parts. You have not done this, nor have I. And on account of our rebellion against God, which is sin, he will punish us for violating the purpose for which we were created" (John 3:36; Romans 1:18-21; Acts 17:30-31; 1 John 3:4).

What I was doing up to this point was reveal who God is and what he is like (i.e., God as Creator and

Judge). I shared his law with them, which is written on their hearts (Romans 2:15). They know what God demands, but as Paul said, they suppress the truth in unrighteousness (Romans 1:18). Remember that the work of his law is written on their hearts. You have allies. Use them! They may neglect or reject these truths, but their conscience testifies differently (Romans 2:15-16).

During this witnessing encounter, I told them that I am a sinner, too, and that I, too, deserved God's wrath and curse. Yet, with an explanation of my terms, I told them that I am saved by grace alone through faith alone and in Christ alone. I did not do anything to deserve this great gift! Therefore, instead of looking down on them for their rebellion against God, I sympathized with them. I wanted them to know that I understand. "But God!"

From the opening words of Genesis to the closing words of Revelation (I had time to share with them; we were flying across the country), I shared the glorious news of Jesus Christ. Though animals were sacrificed in the Old Testament, Jesus Christ was sacrificed in the New Testament (Hebrews 10:1-14). All of history was building to this point, where God would provide a Savior for his people (Matthew 1:21; Luke 24:44-47). And by faith in him, and repentance from sins, Christ's righteousness and everlasting life are available *now* (Mark 1:15; 2 Corinthians 5:17-21; John 6:47-48).

As an aside, I have found that many people present salvation as if it is something *distant*. "If you trust in Christ," they say, "you will be saved from the wrath to come." This is true, but there is more. Salvation presently saves. The wrath of God abides upon sinners now, but by faith and with repentant hearts, that wrath is removed *and* your relationship with the Lord is reconciled now. Union with Christ is now! Justification and adoption is immediate. Sanctification begins now! While these blessings are real *now*, there is more to come—the new heavens and earth.

When the airplane landed, one of the men looked at me and said, "I have never heard it put like that before." They listened to the word of God, surprisingly had no objections, and departed pleasantly. I don't know what happened to those men. They lived in another area. But they did hear the good news. Perhaps somewhere along the way God opened their eyes and they are part of a Bible-believing church.

Conclusion

As you continue to practice personal evangelism, it will get easier. While your fears may not go away completely, your familiarity with the flow of conversation will help build confidence. Questions may arise during the course of conversation. But that, too, will become easier as you gain in experience. Remember that we Christians have much going for us. When we faithfully bring the word of God, we are 100% effective. Don't lose heart! With the gifts that God gave you, he will be sure to use you to share his law and gospel. And though you may tremble while doing it, I hope you will walk away rejoicing.

Discussion Questions

1. To get into a conversation about the law and the gospel, I mentioned asking the question, "May I share what I believe about God?" What are some alternative ways to bring this up?

2. During a witnessing encounter, someone gives you several minutes to talk about your faith. Walk us through what you would say.

3. Sharing the gospel can be a terrifying task; nevertheless, what are some things you have going for you? How does this bring you comfort?

4. Share some of your experiences about past witnessing encounters. What was it like? What were you thinking as you were sharing the good news? How did it end?

5. Read Acts 17:32-34. How did Paul's audience respond? Should you take anything away from this as you engage unbelievers with the law and the gospel?

EIGHT

HOSPITALITY: "ONE-ANOTHERING" WITH THE STRANGER

In his book, *Reaching Out: The Three Movements of the Spiritual Life*, Henri J. M. Nouwen writes, "Hospitality means primarily the creation of free space where the stranger can enter and become a friend instead of an enemy. Hospitality is not to change people, but to offer them space where change can take place."[10] Elsewhere he says, "If there is any concept worth restoring to its original depth and evocative potential, it is the concept of hospitality."[11]

My term for this type of hospitality is "one-anothering." My wife and I regularly invite members of our church into our home to share a meal, to pray

---

[10] Henri J. M. Nouwen, *Reaching Out: The Three Movements of the Spiritual Life* (Colorado Springs: Image, 1986), 71.

[11] Nouwen, *Reaching Out*, 66.

together, and get to know each other. Of course there other ways of practicing hospitality (Genesis 18), but this is a method we have embraced. Virtually every moment of "one-anothering" is a blessing. We learn so much about others—discovering their gifts and talents, strengths and weaknesses, hobbies, likes and dislikes. This serves to strengthen our time together on Sunday—the Lord's Day.

You understand. Time that is shared in each other's homes, or even outside the home, serves to strengthen relationships. By extending a gracious hand of hospitality, we obey the Lord. Peter exhorts us in this way: "Above all, keep loving one another earnestly, since love covers a multitude of sins. *Show hospitality* to one another without grumbling" (1 Peter 4:8-9, *italics mine*). Paul adds: "Contribute to the needs of the saints and seek to show hospitality" (Romans 12:13). The case is clear. Christians are commanded to "create a free space" for the sake of mutual encouragement.

Is it easy? It can be, but not necessarily. What is more difficult is "one-anothering" with *the stranger*. A stranger is one whom Nouwen says can enter your home and "become a friend instead of an enemy." Your next-door neighbor, the post office clerk, co-workers, friends of the family, and children's friends—some of these people would welcome more than a customary greeting throughout the week. Will you extend that warm and welcoming hand of hospitality? Will you one-another with them?

Needless to say, this requires courage, as does sharing our faith with strangers. There are many unknowns. One friend described it as a "messy ministry." Indeed, it is messy, especially the way he explained it.

During my time in seminary I had to select a church to join. At the risk of sounding like a consumer, I noticed there were many great churches in the area that faithfully preached the word, administered the sacraments, and conducted church discipline as needed. It came down to visiting each church, seeing how they received my wife, and inquiring into opportunities to serve. At one point, I narrowed down the selection to two churches. In conversation with one of the pastors, I asked him what he thought the differences were between the church he served and the other church I was considering. His response was remarkable.

"Both of our churches preach the word; both of our churches are growing; but we're growing differently," he said. "They are growing largely by transfer growth. We are growing because drug dealers, gangsters, and prostitutes are coming off the street. When we invite them into our homes—even around our children—they cuss, they wear inappropriate clothing. They don't know any better. They eventually come to Christ. The other church's ministry is neat—ours is messy."

No ministry is completely neat and tidy, but as the above comparison shows, one can be messier than another. This pastor and congregation rolled up their sleeves. Their desire was to see the lost come to saving faith in Christ. That meant one-anothering with those in the community—even if they were uncomfortable *sinners*. Read Matthew 11:18-19 and 1 Corinthians 9:19-23.

Our great and perfect example for manifesting superb hospitality is Jesus. He treated *strangers* as family and loved them as himself (Lev. 19:33-34). He offered food, friendship and faith. He extended care when others turned away. He offered companionship to the lonely. He breathed life into dead bodies. Amazingly, he did this for us. "Therefore remember," Paul says, "that at one time you Gentiles in the flesh, called the uncircumcision by what is called the circumcision…were at that time separated from Christ, alienated from the commonwealth of Israel and strangers to the covenants of promise, having no hope of God in the world. But now in Christ Jesus you who once were far off have been brought near by the blood of Christ" (Ephesians 2:11-13).

If gratitude is your response to such great love, then how can you show it? Jesus said, by loving "your neighbor as yourself" (Matthew 22:39). I contend that this command includes one-anothering with *the stranger* (Hebrews 13:1-2). Use your time and resources to get to know people (Luke 14:12-14). "Offer them space where change can take place."

In the Marketplace

When we first moved to Virginia, a priority of mine was to get to know the people in the community. From time to time I walked around the neighborhood surrounding the church and attempted to talk to anyone within earshot. When this method failed to achieve results, simply because when I was at work others were also at work, I looked for another way.

Local coffee houses are great places to meet people and attempt to one-another. I chose one nearest to the church. By being there regularly I could make observations, such as learning who the regulars were, gradually become familiar with them and them with me. I also came to know the employees.

After some time, I decided to interact with one of the employees. By this time we had only exchanged cordial words as I ordered coffee; nevertheless, there was something about this particular fellow that intrigued me. He was friendly; he took his job seriously; his smile lit up the room; he was gay.

June 26, 2013 marked a change in the traditional—and biblically accurate—definition of marriage. Marriage was defined as "a legal union between one man and one woman as husband and wife." The Defense of Marriage Act (DOMA) stated, "…and the word 'spouse' refers only to a person of the opposite sex who is a husband or a wife." Yet the Supreme Court overturned DOMA. The definition of marriage has been stretched. Additionally, where states allow same-sex union, employers can no longer withhold federal benefits.

Blogs, talk shows, newspapers, pastors—everyone has had something to say about the Supreme Court decision. Yet there is something to be said about homosexuals. In fact, you can say the same thing about

135

heterosexuals. Most of them are all *in Adam*. The wrath of God abides upon them (John 3:36). Homosexuals, like heterosexuals, are consumed in their pride, arrogance, and hatred toward God (Ezekiel 16:44-52; Proverbs 6:16-19; 8:13; Romans 8:7). Therefore, they need what I need; they need what you need—*the gospel*.

With this particular employee at the coffee shop, I approached him and asked, "Do you know what I do for a living?" He responded, "No." Replying somewhat playfully, I said, "Guess!" Three tries later, he came up empty. "I am a pastor." "Oh," he replied. That led to a conversation lasting a few days. Every time I saw him at the coffee shop, we continued our conversation.

During one of our talks, I invited him over for a meal. Surprising to me was his response. He said, "I need some guidance in my life." I told him that he could bring whomever he'd like to our home. I wanted him to feel comfortable coming over. It was probably risky enough for him to come to a pastor's home as a homosexual. He had likely read enough and perhaps even heard enough from pastors and Christians about sin and homosexuality. Nevertheless, I wanted to create a space for *the stranger*. I wanted him to be "a friend instead of an enemy." That kind of relationship takes time. Hospitality to *the stranger* provides an avenue for developing that relationship.

With Your Next Door Neighbors

I have a neighbor by the name of Josh. We see each other almost every day. I know what time he arrives home from work; he knows the same of me. From my front door, I can walk to his house in about 80 paces. We are cordial. We talk about the weather, pets, and anything we happen to find we have in common—our children.

We cross these boundaries regularly, but the conversation doesn't deepen. Where is he from? Does he have any siblings? How long has he been married? What are his hobbies? What does his wife enjoy doing? Do they believe in God? We never covered these topics, although I desperately wanted to. But when I wanted to bridge that gap, somehow the conversation was cut short.

Day-by-day, month-by-month, one year later, our relationship remained the same. I knew very little about him. He knew I was a pastor, but that was the extent of his knowledge. We never went for a walk around the neighborhood, gathered our spouses together to get to know each other—nothing. Did I fail? Should I have done something differently? Did my vocation sterilize our relationship?

Reflecting upon what I could have or should have done is always a downward spiral. I don't do anything perfectly. There is always room for improvement. I can say things differently, refrain from saying as much, pray more. And yet despite my shortcomings, God always proves faithful. Throughout the course of my interactions with Josh, I periodically invited his family over for a meal. It has yet to happen.

Sometimes an opportunity to be hospitable doesn't materialize. That doesn't mean we've failed. It simply means it's not time. Perhaps a certain level of comfort must be established with our neighbors before they cross the threshold of our home. For some people, it takes longer; for others, less time.

Despite my attempts to get to know Josh and his family, I received a surprising knock at my door one Sunday evening just days before my family moved out of the neighborhood. Josh heard that I needed my tree trimmed. He volunteered to help. After about 10 minutes of tree conversation, I thought the conversation was at an end. I was wrong. "There's a reason I don't go to church," Josh said. "What?" I thought. I've been trying to get to know you and have this conversation for a year. "Now, Lord?" God's timing is always perfect! We stood in the driveway for an hour talking about God, his reasons for not attending church, and his plans for the future.

Making Those Connections

Regardless of how long you've lived in your neighborhood, there are things you can do to get to know your neighbors better. In an age of Facebook and Twitter you may think you know people fairly well, but nothing replaces face-to-face interaction. There's something to be said for observing body language, eye contact, shared laughter and perhaps even communal tears. "LOL" is not a good substitute for a genuine body-shaking, forehead wrinkling laughter. Emoticons do not supplant a hug when someone is mourning. "IMHO" shouldn't replace sensitive, person-to-person conversations.

With our neighbors and those in the broader community, an old-fashioned approach is the way to get to know them. Facebook and Twitter are fine in their place, but personal interaction will never have a substitute. Engage your neighbor. See how they're doing. Find out what is new in their lives. Inquire about their well-being. This can occur over a meal or during an extended conversation in the driveway.

Be mindful, however, when you're making those connections, don't do so as a smoke screen to help reduce your fears so that when you eventually have the opportunity to share the gospel, it becomes less of a burden. People are intelligent. They know whether you're truly interested in them. Inquire about their well-being because you love them. Sharing the gospel should be a natural byproduct, although there will be times when you are able to share the gospel immediately.

Plan a barbeque and invite your neighbors. If you walk every morning, ask a neighbor if they'd like to come along. Consider starting a book club and send out invitations. If there are needs being unmet, see what you can do to help. Get to know the local grocery store workers, post office clerks, and gas station attendants. The list of possible ways and means is long.

The bottom line in all of this is to do it—to do something—and to be diligent and devoted to it. We must be diligent. We are busy people. It is tough to carve out additional time for others—for *the stranger*. But difficult is not impossible. We may have to incorporate lifestyle changes (e.g., rearranging schedules, removing some extracurricular activities, etc.). Yet the blessings that come from loving our neighbors and being hospitable outweigh our momentary inconveniences and scheduling changes.

Be Safe and Smart

Hospitality can be dangerous. Inviting a stranger into your home may be a risk to your family. A dear friend and chaplain in the navy used to invite homeless people to stay overnight at his home. This afforded him with opportunity to minister to them. When he and his wife began having children, he stopped. Although nothing harmful happened, he thought it wise for the safety of his children to refrain from such hospitality. He now expresses hospitality in other ways.

Of course not every opportunity should be acted on. Wisdom and discernment should determine the extent of hospitality. Men should not place themselves in compromising positions with women and vise versa. Prayer is vital to the task. Ask the Lord to grant wisdom as you seek to be hospitable to *the stranger*.

As a married man, I don't want to send the wrong message. If I am speaking with a woman, I immediately share that I'm married, and that it would be a delight for me, *as well as my wife*, to get to know her better, leaving it to my wife to make the decisive invitation.

Perhaps meeting with another family or individual is more suitable in a public place. Your options are many if you decide to meet publicly. Restaurants, parks, public libraries, and coffee shops are good places to meet. It may be less threatening to meet in a public place for both parties.

Whatever you do and wherever you do it, your welcoming and loving embrace to *the stranger* will hopefully bring great delight to their day. And as you get to know people, it will also give you great joy. Learning about another person in a meaningful way is truly a blessing. As you do so, may the Lord grant you opportunities to share your faith, as you "love your neighbor as yourself."

Conclusion

Hospitality is a key ingredient to becoming better acquainted with people. In a time when busyness often rules our lives, let us take time for *the stranger*. We are easily content in our quaint spheres of influence—our church families and our own families. But when we water the thirsty hearts of our neighbors, they will blossom as their roots sink deep into their new friendship with you. Hospitality provides a way to get to know the stranger. It means "the creation of free space where the stranger can enter and become a friend instead of an enemy." And by God's grace, this will open the window of opportunity to talk about Christ and his Church.

Discussion Questions

1. How did Jesus Christ demonstrate the ultimate act of hospitality for you?

2. What are some of the difficulties associated with one-anothering with the stranger? How will you navigate those difficulties?

3. Do you currently know people in your community with whom you'd like to be hospitable? How will you go about extending hospitality to them?

4. What are some ways you can be smart and safe as you attempt to show hospitality to those in your community?

5. Describe a time when you one-anothered with someone in your community. How did it go? What were some of your fears? How was it a blessing?

NINE

MY PRAYER FOR YOU: SOME PARTING WORDS

My hope at this point is that you are encouraged. My desire is to equip Christians, at a basic level, with some of the ins and outs of personal evangelism. This book was not primarily written for those who are already bold witnesses, but for those who struggle with where to start, what to read, where to go for help, the importance of the Church as a witness or how to remain active in sharing your faith. After teaching many Sunday school classes on this topic, I realized many people wanted more. Forty-five minutes in a Sunday school lesson on personal evangelism was not enough. For them I wrote this book.

Allow me some final thoughts by way of conclusion.

My Prayer Bench

Over the years I have struggled with consistency in prayer. I have tried to improve. For a time, I set my alarm clock 30 minutes earlier than I would normally get up. This worked for a while. I got up early, retreated to the guest bedroom, and prayed. I thought this method would keep me vibrant in prayer for the rest of my life. However, when my schedule changed, my prayer routine changed. I moved from praying in solitude in the guest bedroom to praying in solitude while I was driving.

I then tried carving certain times into my schedule throughout the day that would allow me to take breaks to pray. Since my schedule varied, I had to vary my prayer schedule each day. At certain times, my alarm sounded and I prayed. Sometimes I went for a walk as I prayed, and at other times I prayed where I was. This, too, ended sooner than I intended. Like a New Year's resolution, it only lasted so long. When it was time to pray, I had other things pressing that *seemed* to require immediate attention. "I will pray when I am done," I thought. I kept pushing it back until I realized I had only met one of those scheduled prayer times.

Some years later I was being considered for a pastoral call. Most churches seeking a pastor would naturally inquire about personal prayer. I said I struggled with consistency. Thankfully, they were not looking for a perfect man and decided to issue a call. When I arrived, I asked the deacons if the budget allowed for the purchase of a prayer bench. I later found a box in front of my study with a prayer bench inside. Placed next to my desk, I cannot come into my study without being reminded of the need to pray. The bench has helped a great deal. This is the most consistent I have been in prayer. I finally found something that works.

The purpose of sharing this story is to reveal how I have tried to stay consistent in an area where I am weak. *Consistency* is one of the war cries of the Christian life. And it becomes more apparent where we struggle the most.

Is personal evangelism one area where you need to shout the war cry? Do you invite others to church and share the gospel consistently? Despite how fearful you are and how uncomfortable you find yourself, do you set those struggles aside for the greater good—the salvation of sinners? If you struggle with consistency in personal evangelism as I do with prayer, is there a "prayer bench" of personal evangelism that can remind you of the need? Of course no physical object can replace a heart driven by the gospel to witness to a lost and dying world. But sometimes a visible reminder helps.

My Prayer for You

I pray that you will not be discouraged. I know sharing the good news and inviting others to church are difficult. Sometimes we think we are not cut out for this task. Others seem more gifted and handle themselves in their evangelistic endeavors with greater ease. "Why can't we be like them?" we think. Or we say, "If only I had it like them, I would share my faith more."

Don't compare yourself with others. God renewed you in the image of the Son, and he made you unique! He has given you certain gifts to use for his kingdom. What you have to do is put them into practice in personal evangelism. At the expense of sounding like a basketball coach, "You can do it!" Instead of wishing you were like the next guy, use that person as an instrument of encouragement. Sharing the gospel and inviting others to church is tough enough. Don't let personas of others weigh you down.

My prayer also is that you will remain motivated. You may not see fruit immediately. You are inviting people to church, sharing the gospel consistently, and none of those people are darkening the doorstep of your church or responding to God's call to repent and place one's faith in Christ. Is it worth it? Is this effective? Is it a waste of time?

These questions spring from doubt. Think about what you are doing. You are sharing the greatest message in the world. Is it worth it? Is it effective? Of course it is! God's word does not return void. Additionally, you may be sharing the gospel with a person who has never heard it. It is not a waste of time. God requires that you share the good news. It is a privilege! Even if you do not see fruit, stay motivated. The farmer keeps planting year after year. God is at work. Trust that he will work it out according to his good will.

When we first moved to Virginia, it was a definite change from Southern California. People wave to passers by as they drive down the street. There is a warmth and friendliness that is different from the West Coast. Another difference is the number of churches. Church here is clearly more a way of life. On Sunday mornings, church parking lots are full, driveways are empty, and many stores are closed. It seems that everyone goes to church.

So when I started conversations with people about church, many responded that they already attend. My next question, "Where do you attend?" was often answered just as quickly. Since I did not want to take people from other churches to attend mine, I'd end with, "That is great!" or I shared the gospel with them because, as Christians, the gospel should be an enormous encouragement. Later on I then began to approach things differently. I started to understand the culture and realized that because people say they go to church, does not mean that they attend regularly. After finding out which church they went to, I would ask, "When was the last time you went?" This key unlocked the door. Many people confessed that they had not attended in years. With the door opened I would share the gospel and invite them to *my* church.

Still, in all my encounters, people were friendly. No one was hostile toward the gospel. In fact, when I gave them an invitation card to our church, most said that they would attend. Yet rarely did any of them follow up with a visit. Apparently southern hospitality also means that they did not want to hurt my feelings. Saying "no" to an invitation to church might be construed as impolite.

This realization saddened and upset me. At least in Southern California when people said they would come to church, they came. If they were uninterested, they would tell me. Not so in my area of Virginia. But that did not stop me. Since I lived in the community, I continued to see the same people. I continued to strike up similar conversations about Christ and his Church. Gradually persistence and consistency paid off. Eventually some of those people came to church. And that, in part, provided the motivation to keep going. My prayer is that you do not lose heart but press on even when it seems like people are uninterested.

My prayer is that you will receive support from your local church. It is an encouragement to know that your church officers and congregational members are praying for you. Prayer support goes a long way. In fact, as they pray for you, they may be encouraged to share their faith more frequently as well. It can grind on you to pray for someone when you know you are not doing the very thing for which you are praying.

I also pray that your pastor encourages the congregation to invite others to church and share the gospel, and that his encouragement is reinforced by his actions. As the old saying goes, "Like father, like son." The same can be said for churches: "Like pastor, like parishioners." If the pastor has no concern for sharing the gospel outside of Sunday, it is likely that the church will have no concern. But when the pastor emphasizes the importance of sharing the gospel, is consistent in his personal evangelistic efforts, and teaches on the topic, the parishioners begin to see the significance of this endeavor and desire to emulate him.

Lastly, my prayer is that you would remember and further embrace the work of Christ. Without the person and work of Jesus Christ, there would be no Church. Without the person and work of Jesus Christ, the Church would have no Great Announcement and no Great Commission. Without the person and work of Jesus Christ, there would be no gospel to share and no hope at all. The gospel is not merely for converting sinners, but also for sanctifying and edifying Christians.

The apostle Paul says, "...God shows his love for us in that while we were still sinners, Christ died for us" (Romans 5:8). Although you were dead in your trespasses and sins (Ephesians 2:1), God had mercy on you. Jesus Christ, who was fully God and fully man, lived a life of complete perfection. He was tempted in all ways yet without sin (Hebrews 4:15). He voluntarily laid down his life, going to the cross to be crucified, having the wrath of his Father poured upon him in the process. Then he rose from the grave three days later. He finally commissioned his disciples, appeared to many witnesses, and ascended to heaven. He did all of this *for us*. Christ received the wrath of God that we deserve and he lived a perfect life in our place. Now there is therefore no condemnation for those who are in Christ Jesus (Romans 8:1).

Good news comes along occasionally. Great news is more rare. Amazing, life changing news is ours exclusively to share. It is on the basis of Christ that the Church has the privilege to witness. God has saved us from the penalty of sin, so that we can be a part of the work of saving others. All of this is ultimately for God's glory; for the building of his Church; and for the coming of his kingdom.

Are you willing to be used of God as a vessel to invite others to church and to share the good news of salvation? Taking the time to read this book says much about your desire to do so. May you become and remain consistent, motivated, and receive the support of your church along the way. To God be the glory, both now and forever more.

Discussion Questions

1. How can you remain motivated and consistent in inviting others to church and sharing the gospel?

2. Do you foresee becoming discouraged as you seek to invite others to church and share the gospel? How can you overcome this?

3. Think back to chapter five. Why is prayer important in personal evangelism?

4. Take a moment to pray. Among many things, pray that God would use you in your evangelistic endeavors and that he would keep you consistent, motivated, and free from discouragement. Also pray that the Spirit of God would continue to open your eyes to the depths of his grace that is given to you.

Made in the USA
Charleston, SC
26 August 2016